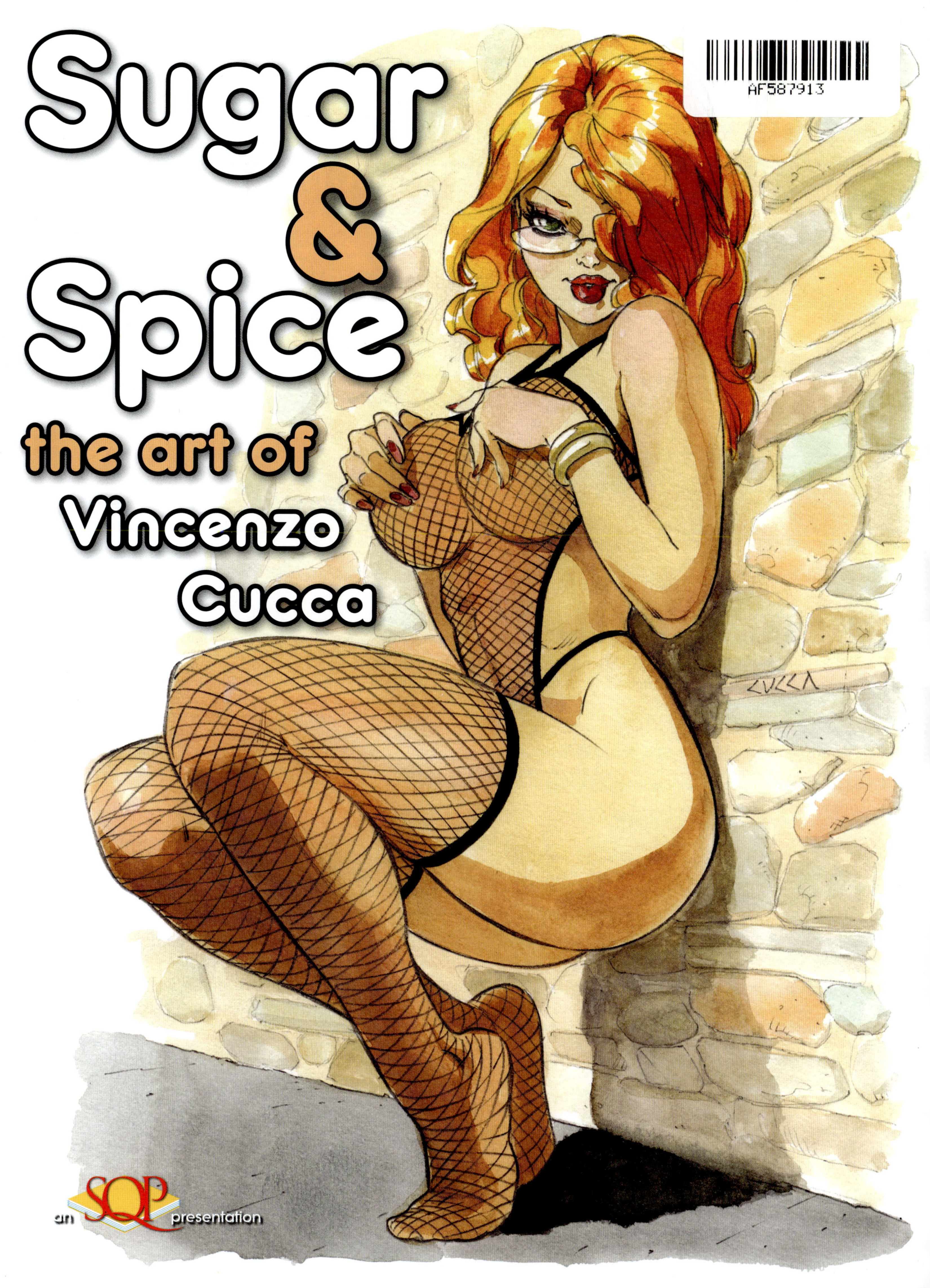
Sugar
&
Spice
the art of
Vincenzo
Cucca
CUCCA
an SQP presentation

and everything nice...

Vincenzo Cucca and the art of making friends one illustration at a time.

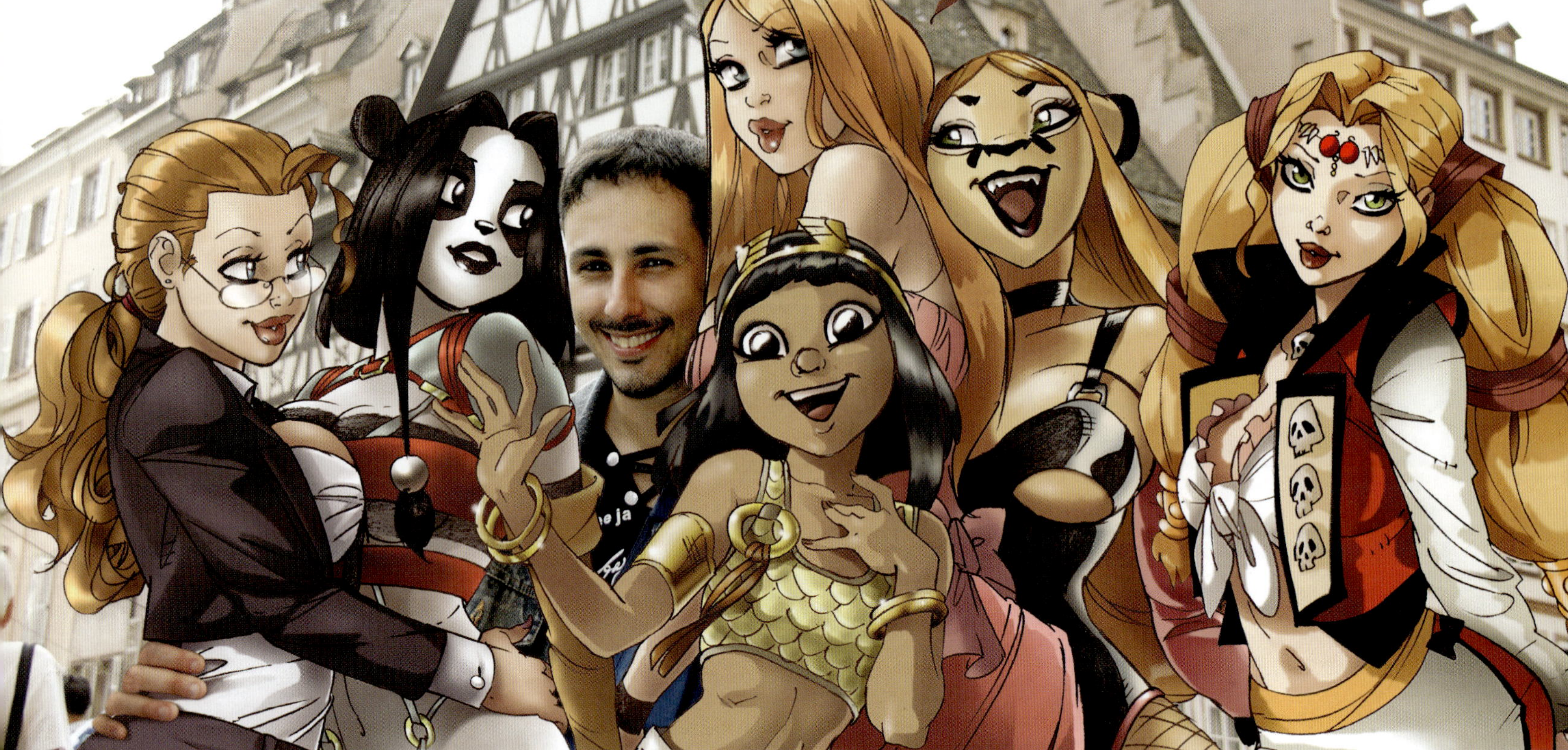

Vincenzo Cucca is Italian, so it's only natural he has a fascination with beautiful women. Fortunately for the rest of us, he can translate that affection in every one of his illustrations.

Born in 1977 in Naples, Italy, Vincenzo showed a talent for drawing which led him on a path that would eventually see him graduate from art school and train at the School of Naples. From there, he worked at various advertising agencies and sculpting workshops, honing his techniques and creating his own unique style.

Starting in 1998, Cucca began working for various comic companies both in Europe and America, slowly building up a portfolio of projects that would generate a following of fans who enjoyed his clean and supple designs.

Cucca has illustrated for Marvel and Disney, Aspen Comics, Glasshouse Graphics and Zenoscope to name just a few, but it's his work on *Pandamonia* and *Hot Charlotte* which he's widely regarded for. That's the focus we wanted to take in this collection appropriately titled "Sugar & Spice". His cartoon creations are both sexy and seductive, sweet with just enough heat to set them apart from all the rest. This gallery of girl-filled goodness will give you a clear indication just how talented Vincenzo is.

As well as an artist and sculptor, Cucca also teaches at the International School of Comics in Pescara, getting the next generation of illustrators ready to follow their passions. The artist also works on commissioned pieces for his many fans. If you enjoy what you see in this book, you can get your very own Cucca original by contacting him via:

cuccadesign.deviantart.com

Sugar & Spice - The Art of Vincenzo Cucca

Book design by Grassy Knoll Studios.

Published by SQP Inc.
PO Box 248 - Columbus NJ 08022

Sal Quartuccio & Bob Keenan - Publishers

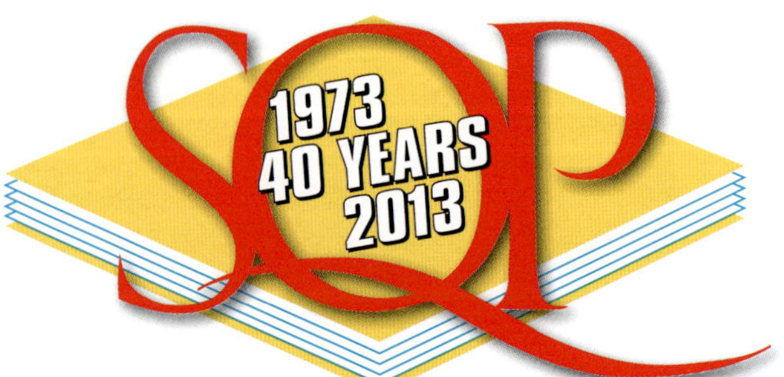

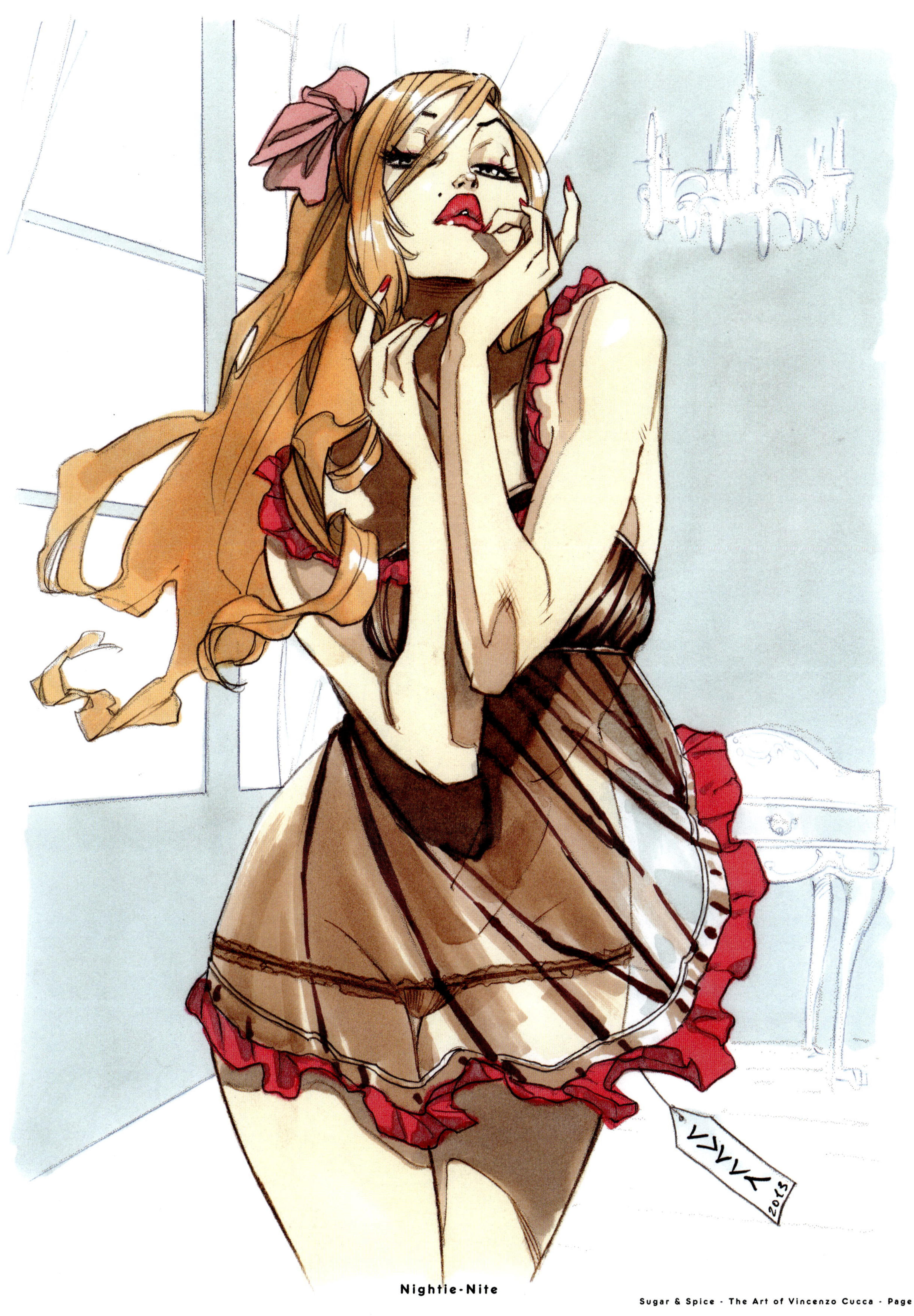

Nightie-Nite

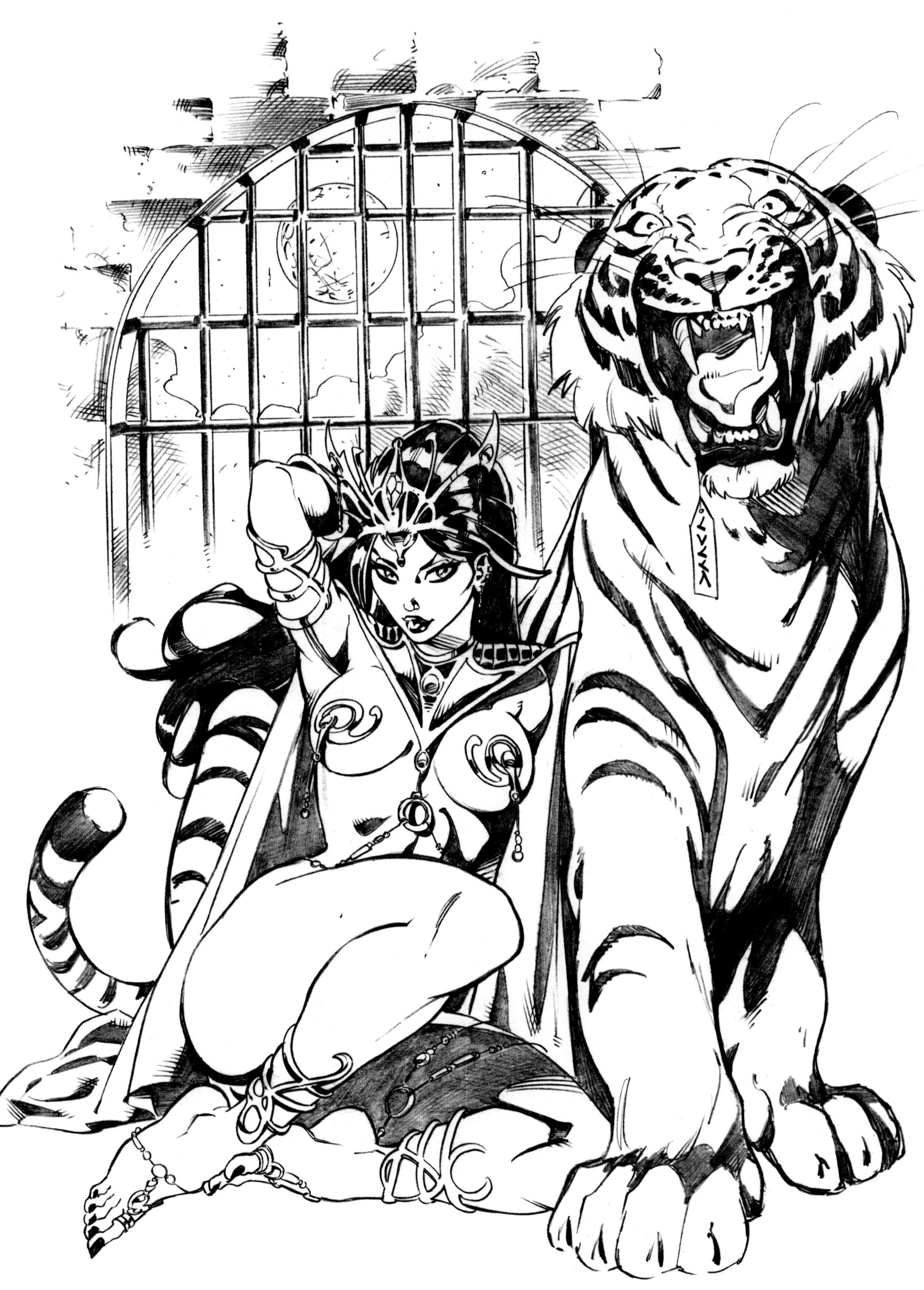

The Beauty of Mars

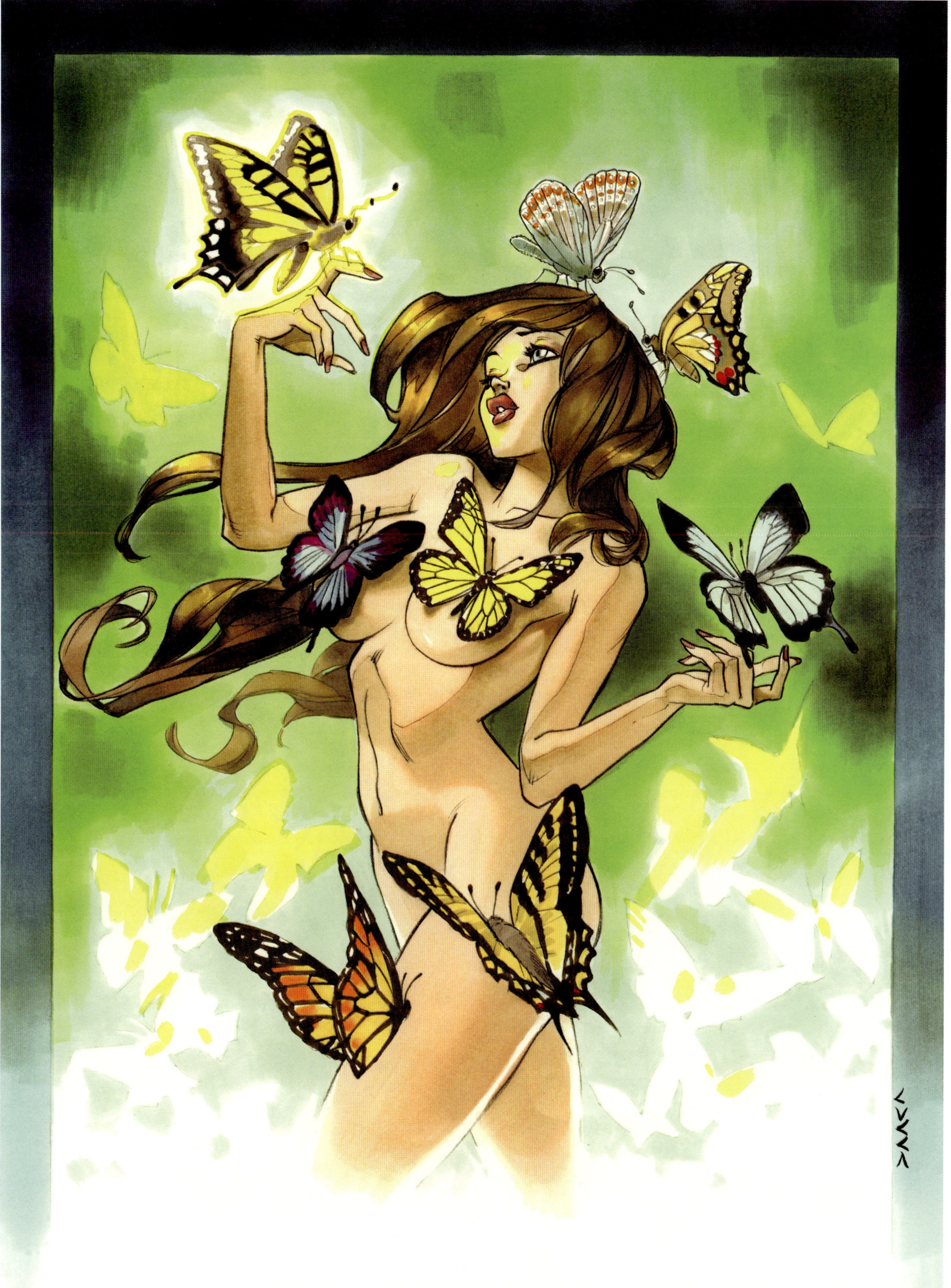

Butterfly Kisses

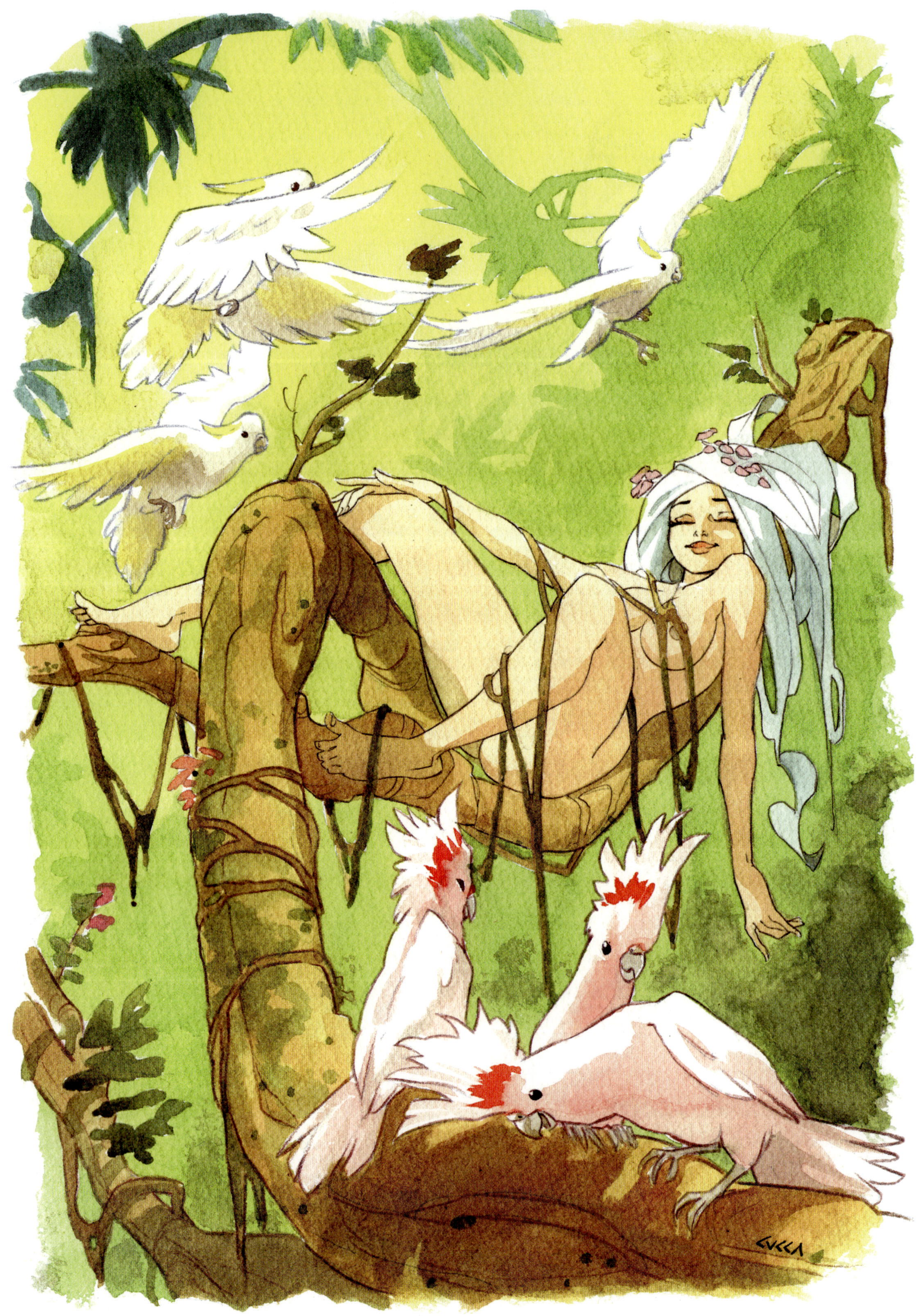

Jungle Rest

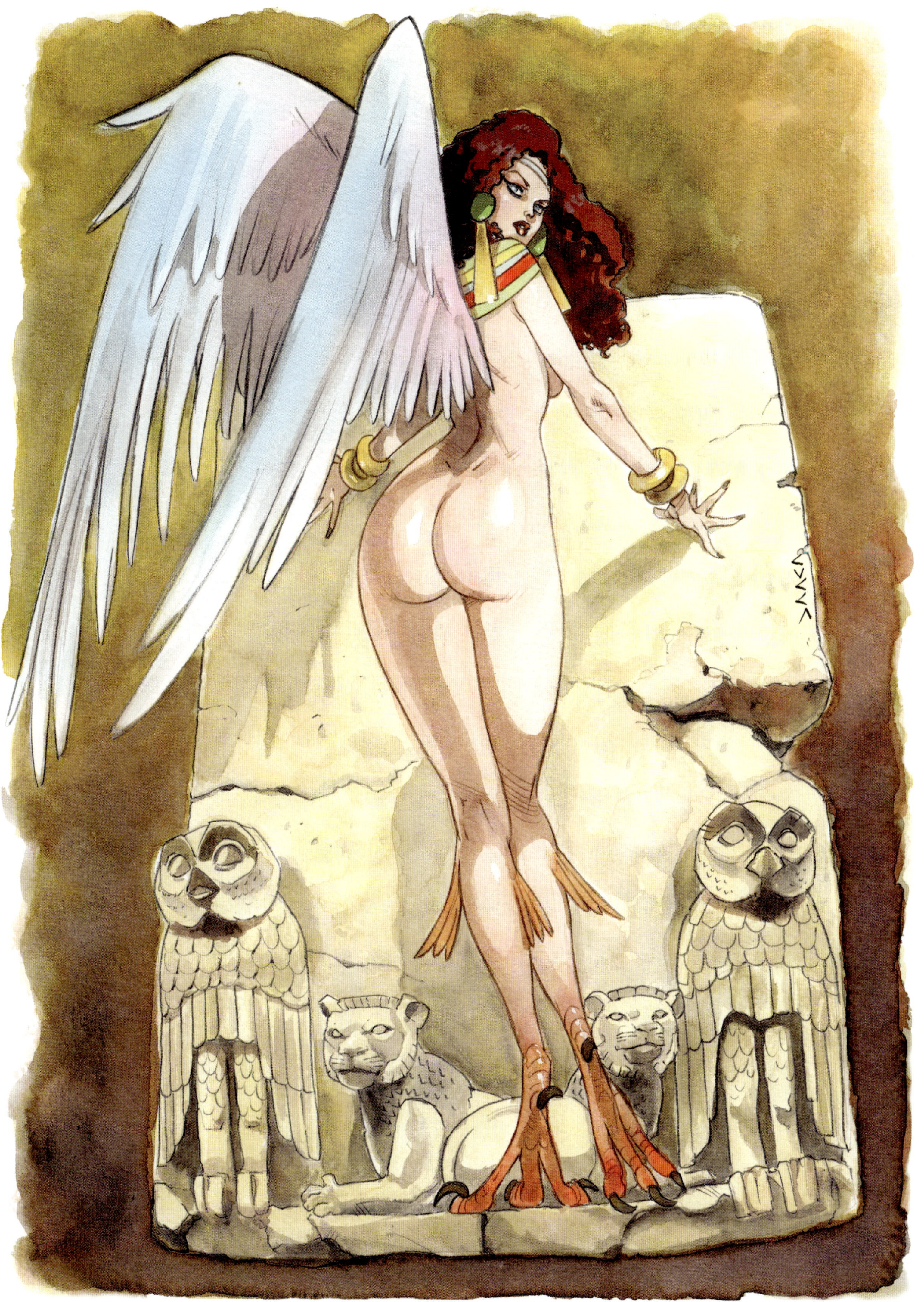

Exquisite Creature

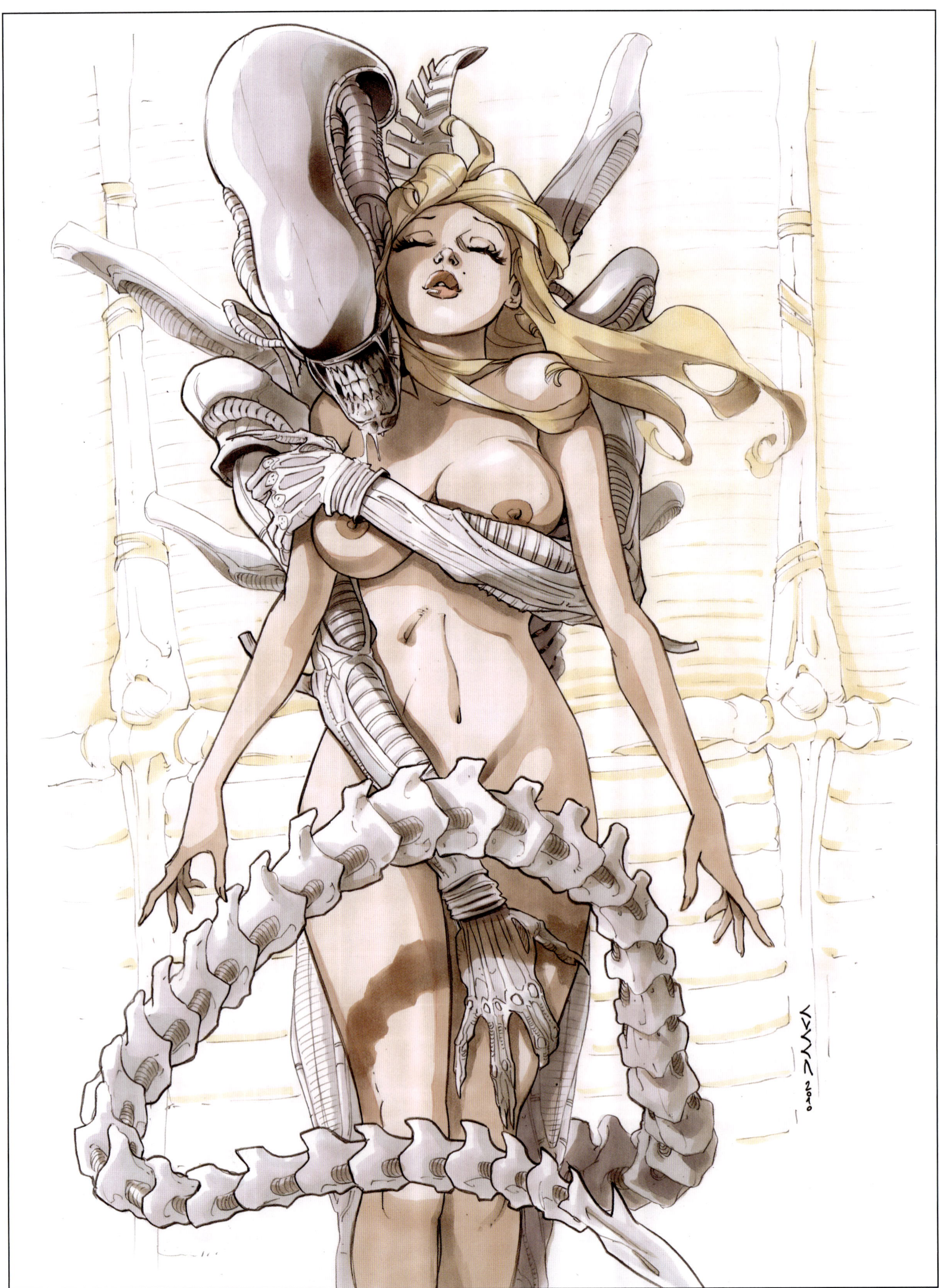

Alienation

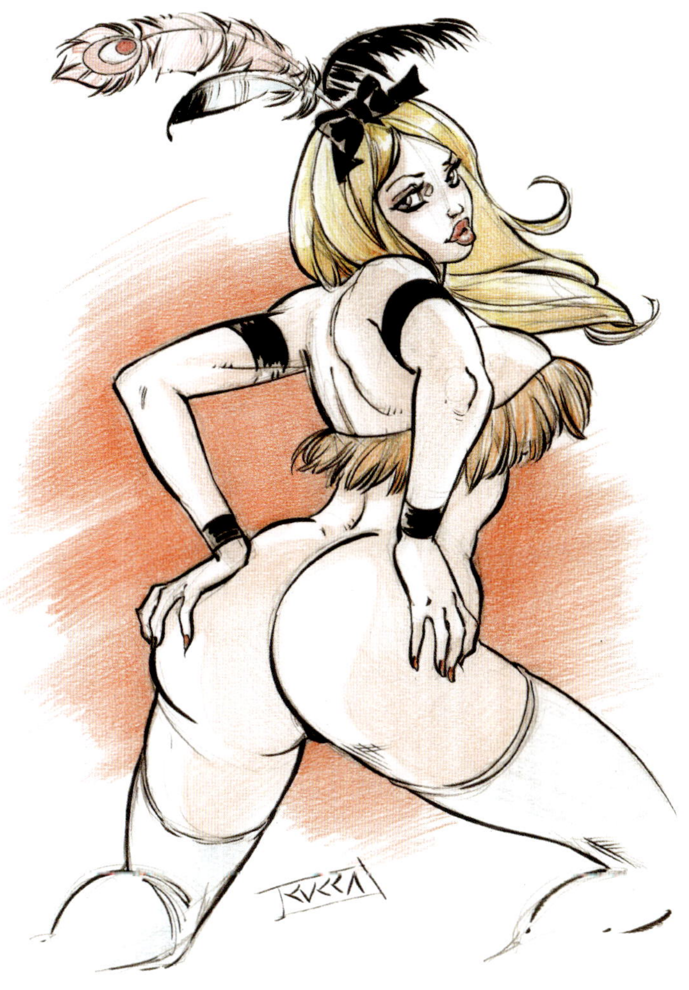

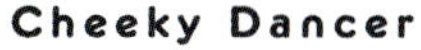

Cheeky Dancer

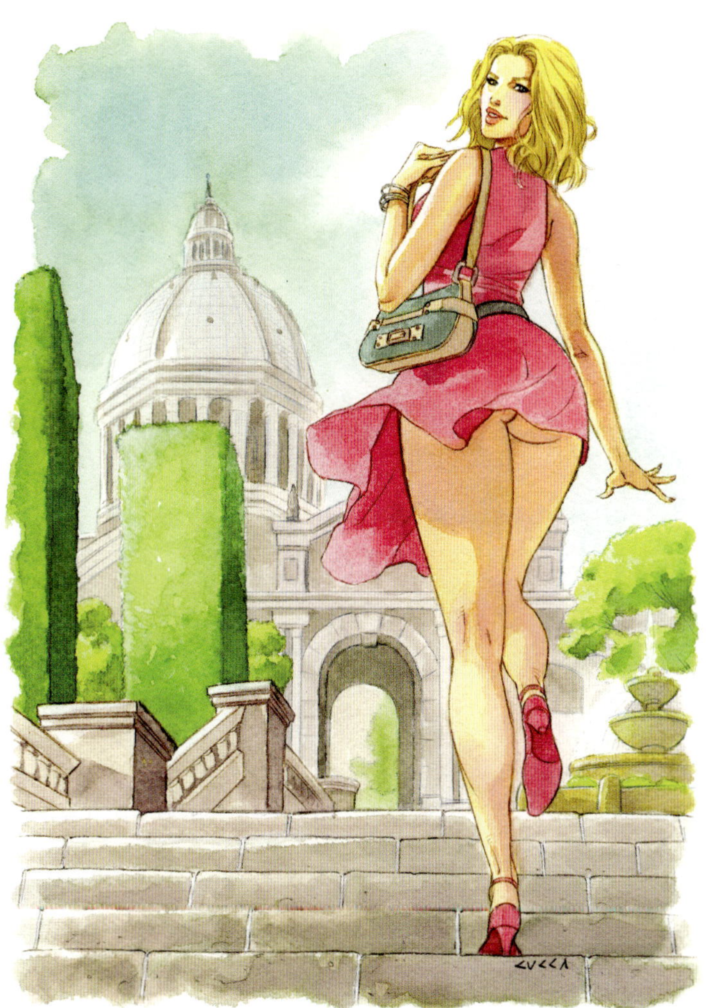

Magnificent View

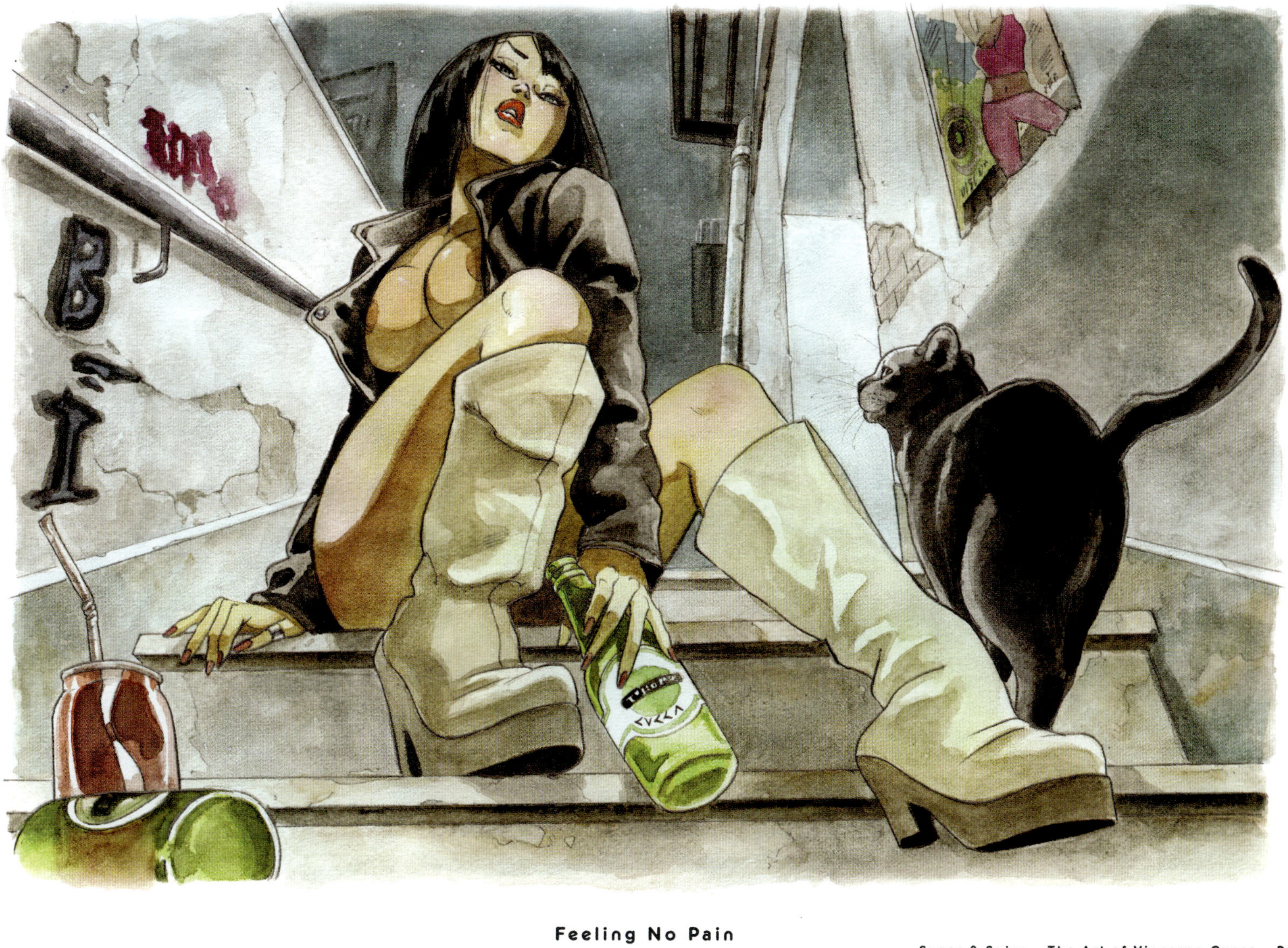

Feeling No Pain

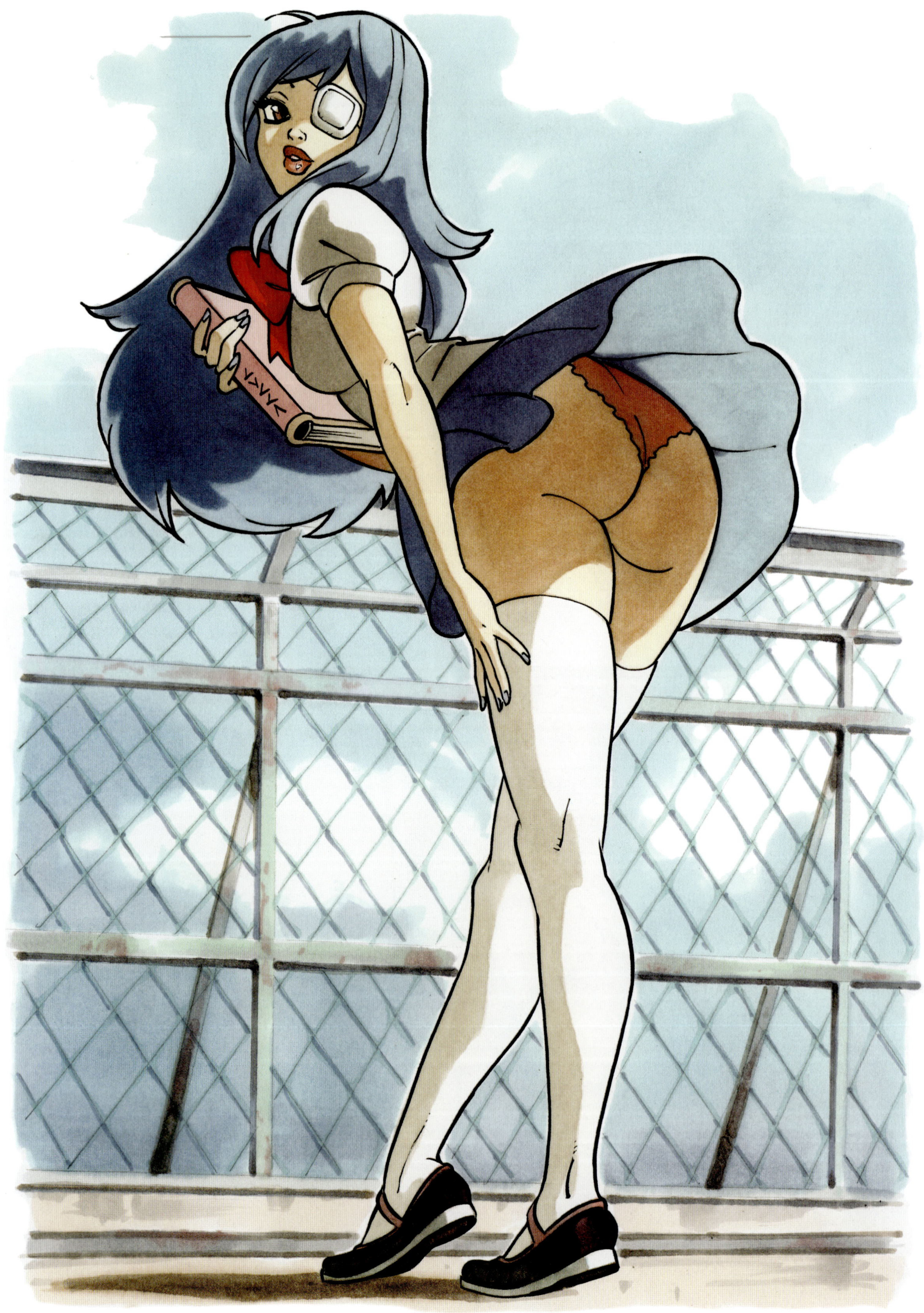

Windy Daze

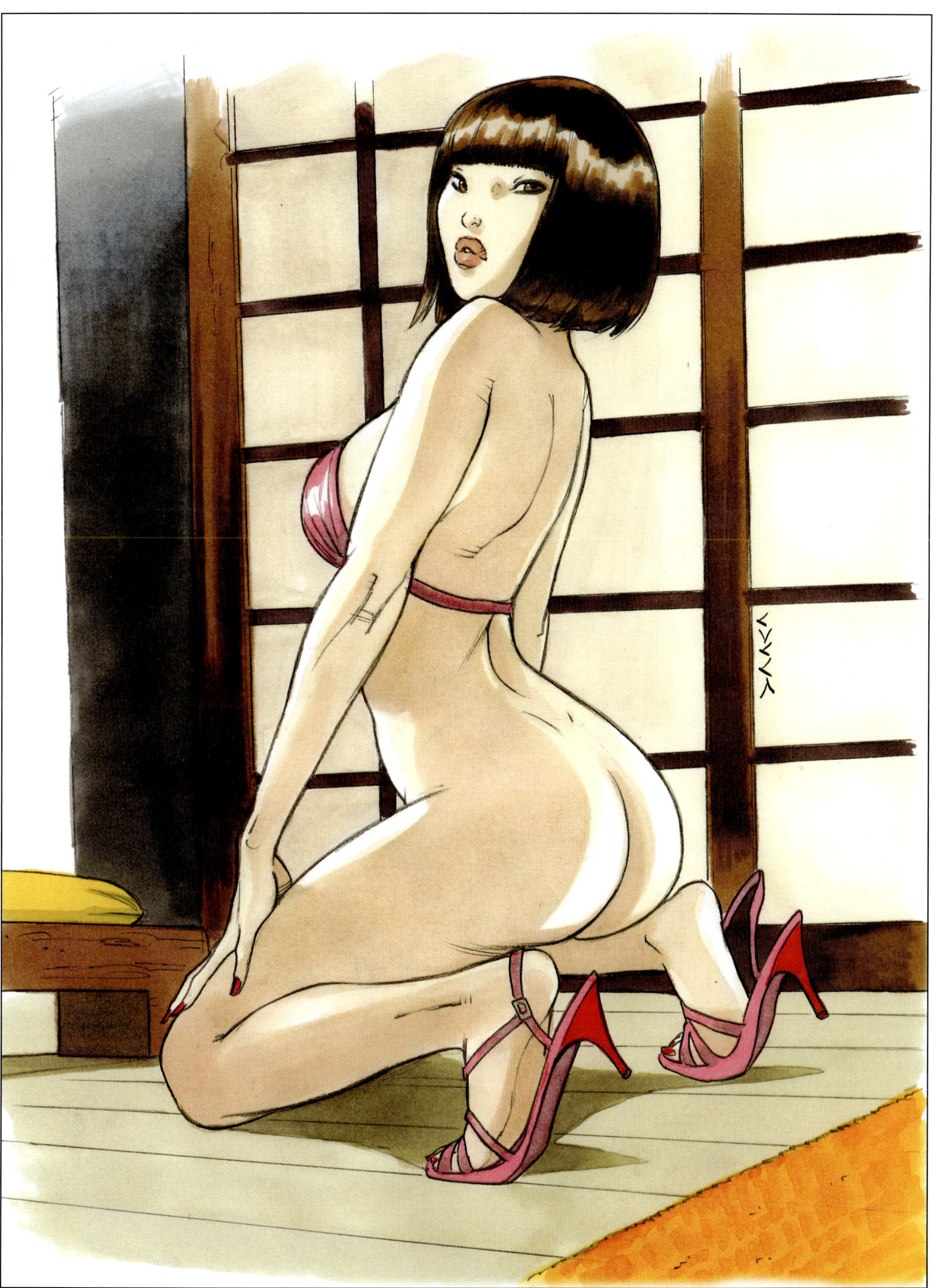

Japanese Dream

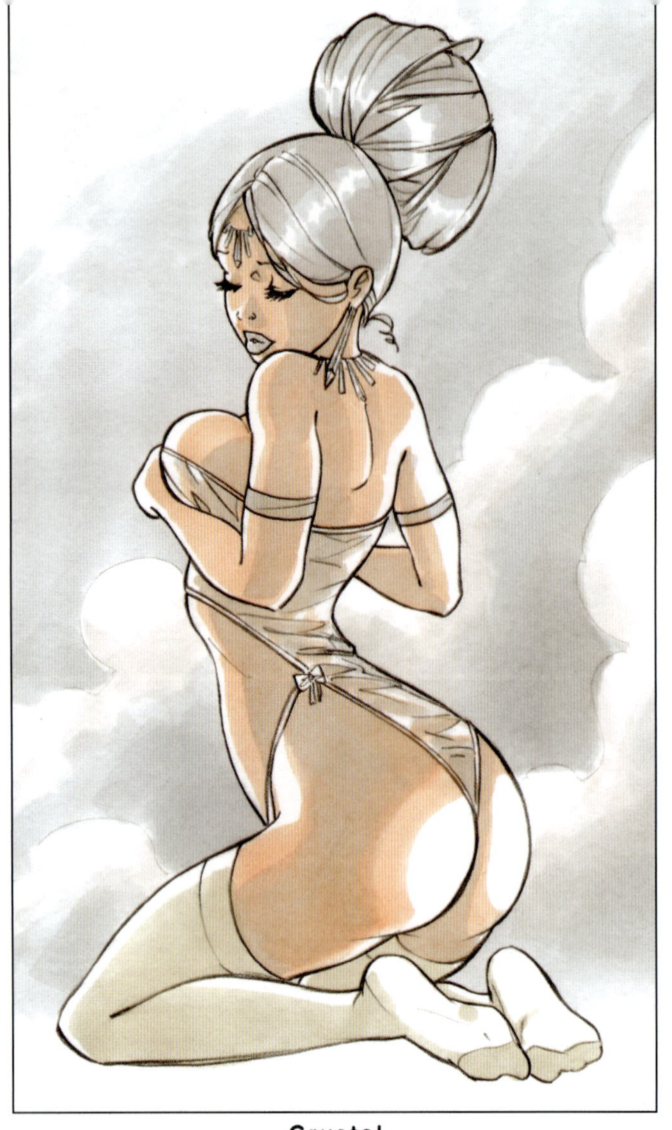

Crystal

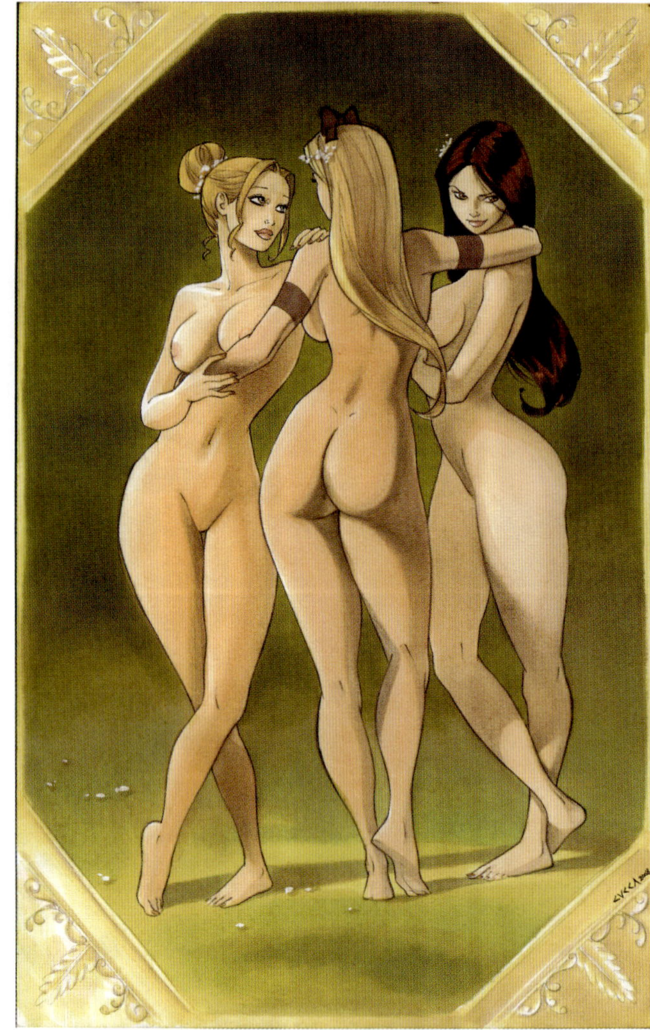

The Three Graces

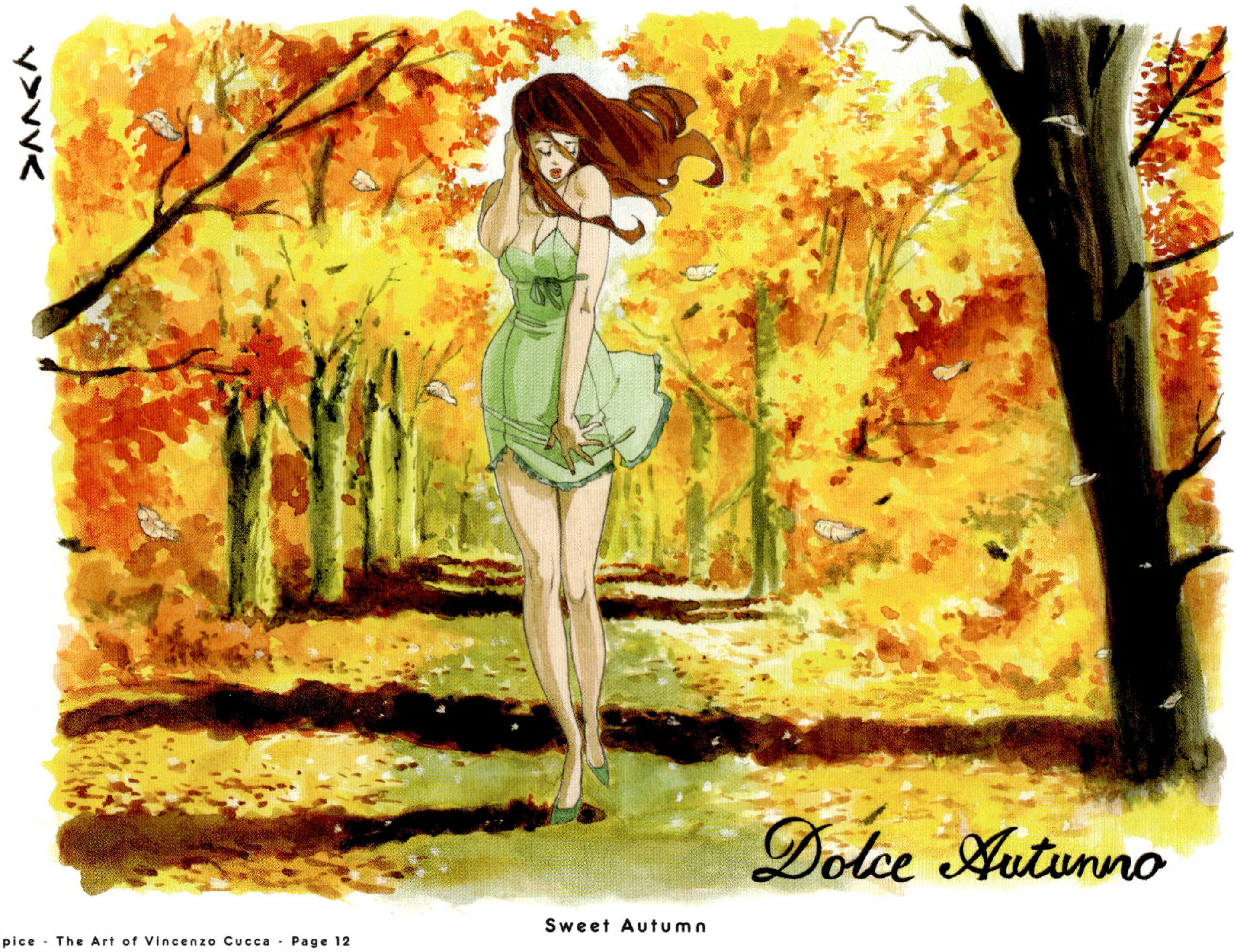

Sweet Autumn

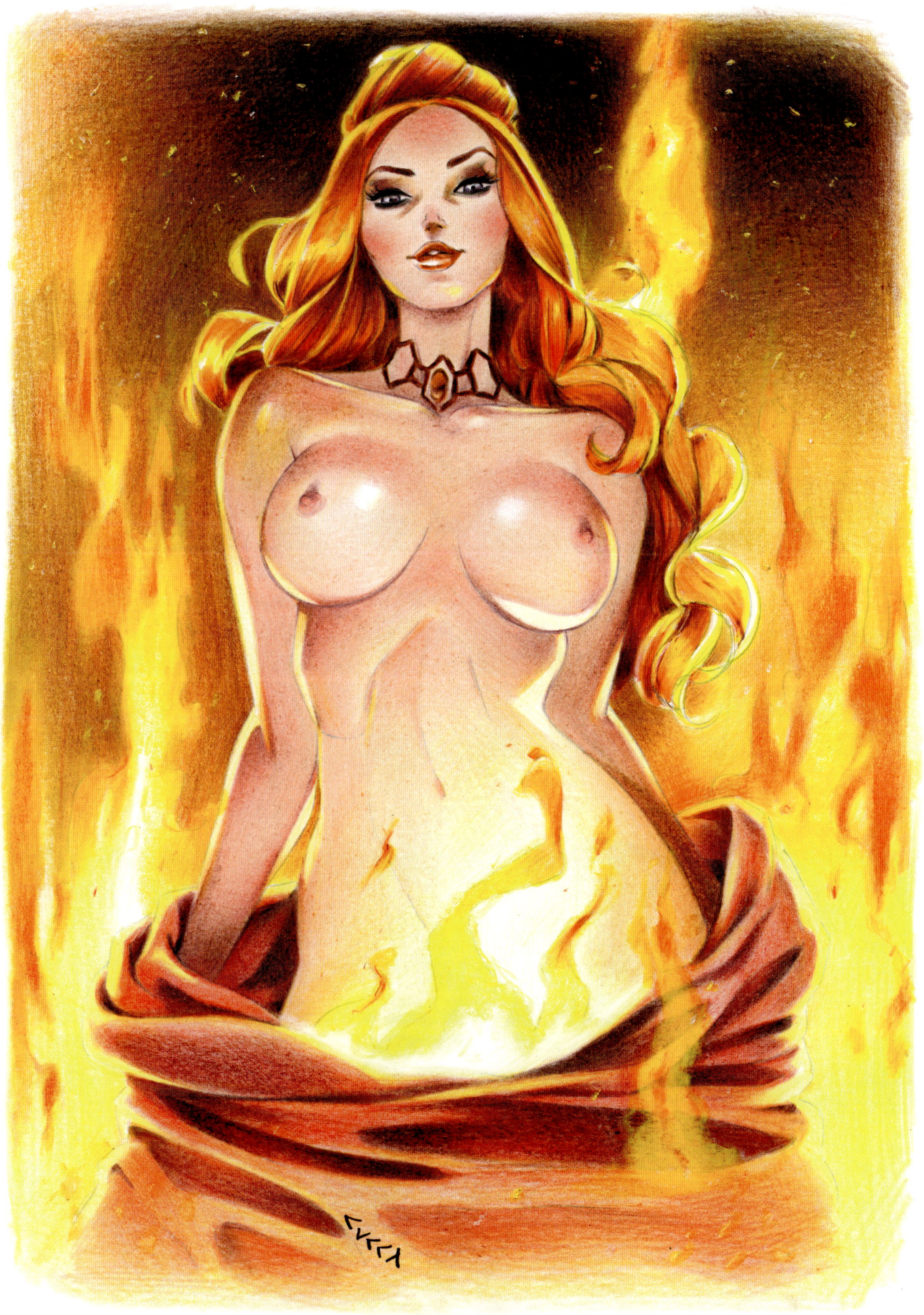

The Red Queen

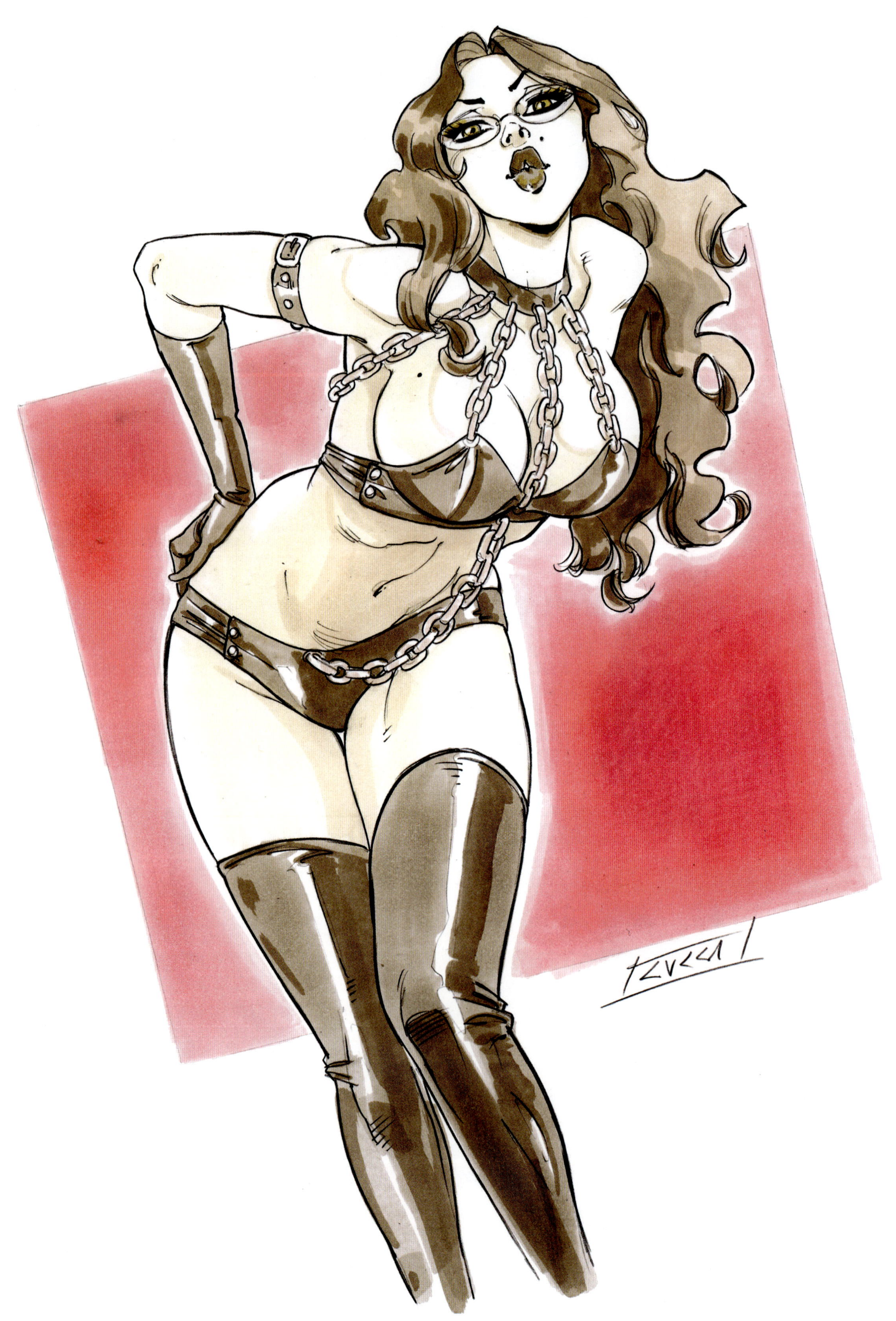

Yes Mistress

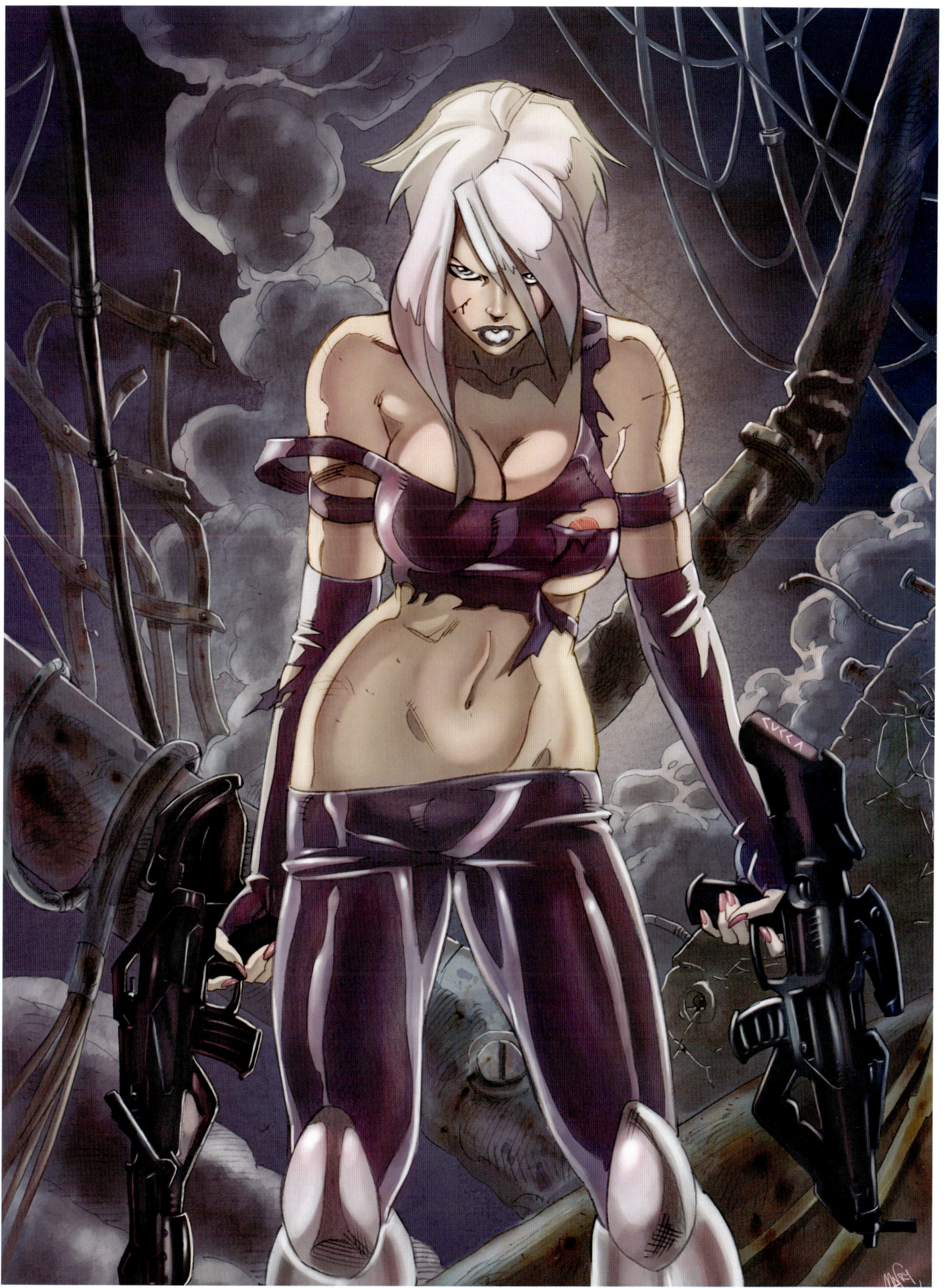

Termite Bianca (color by Mariacristina Federico)

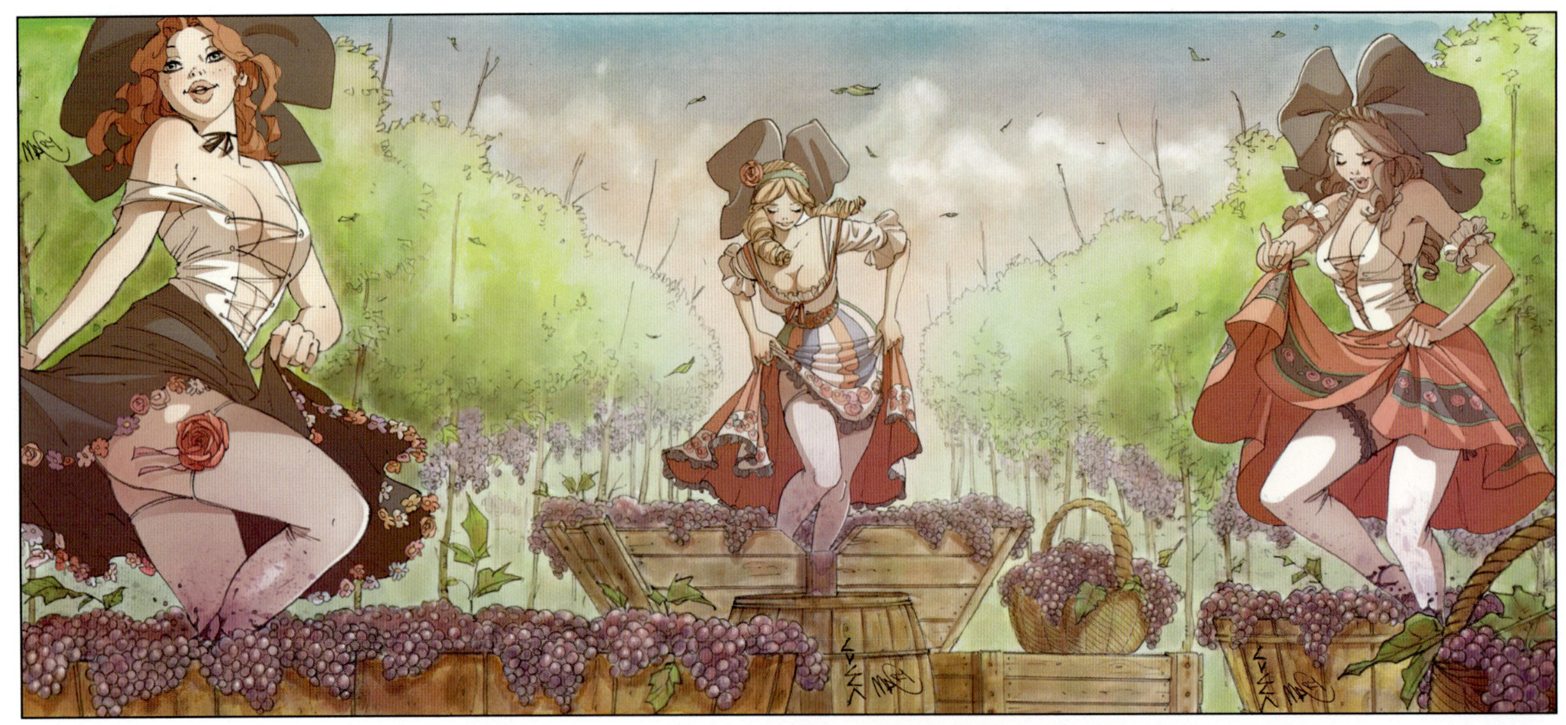

A Memorable Vintage (color by Mariacristina Federico)

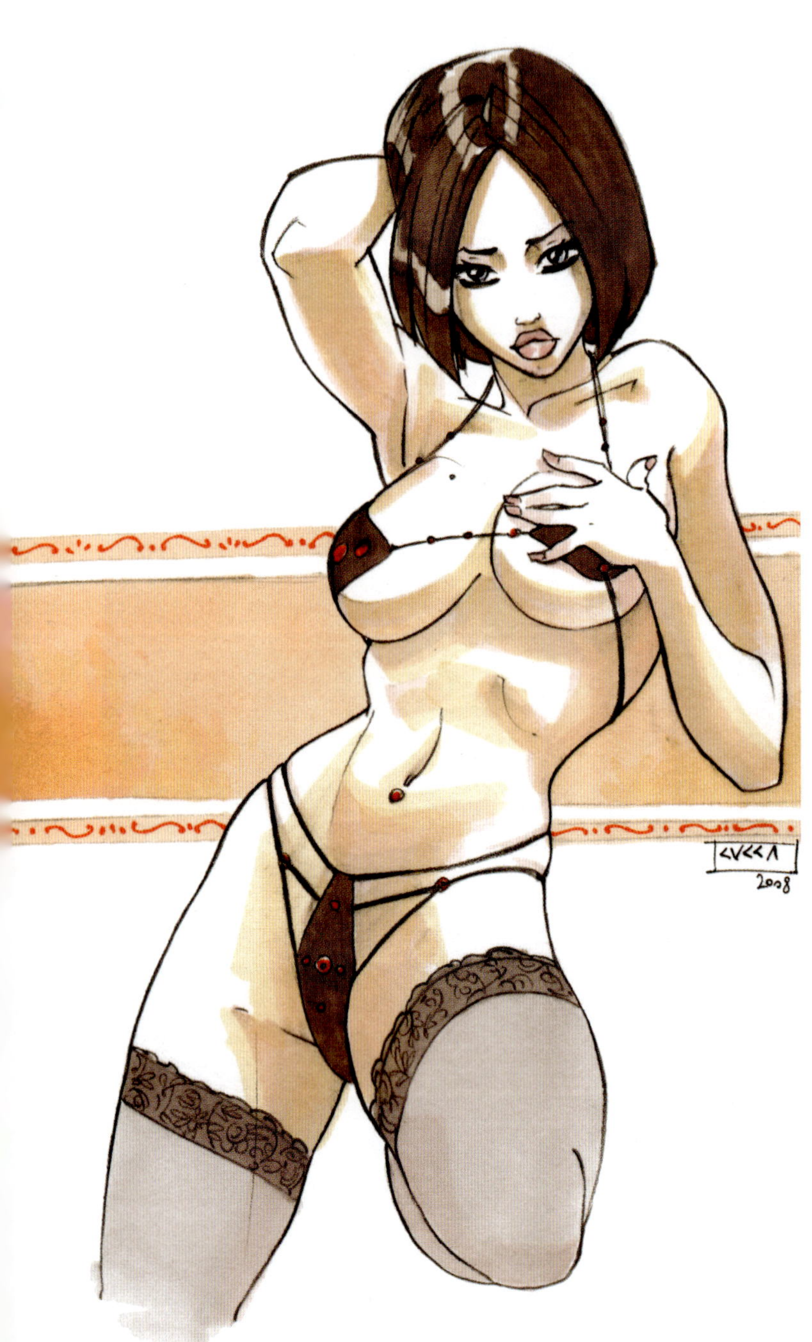

Dangerous Curves

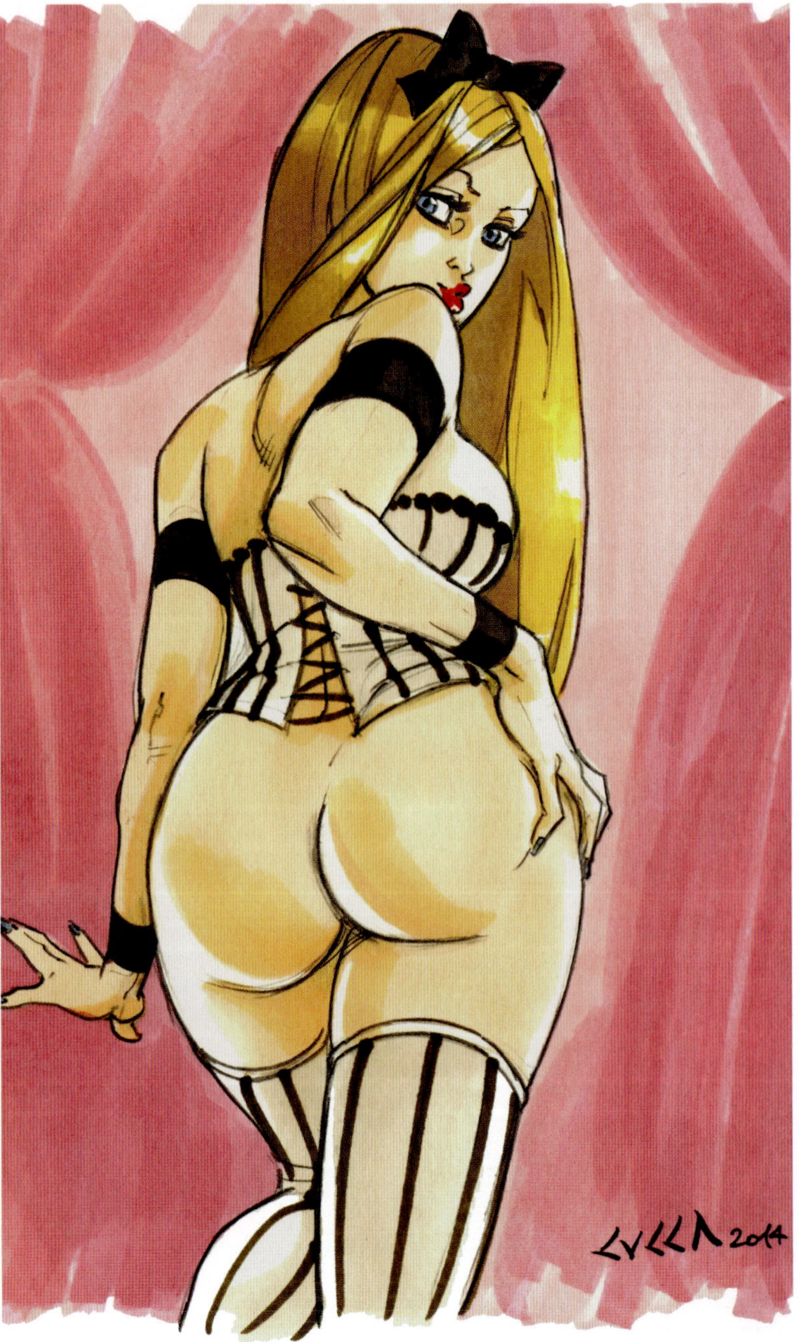

Invitation

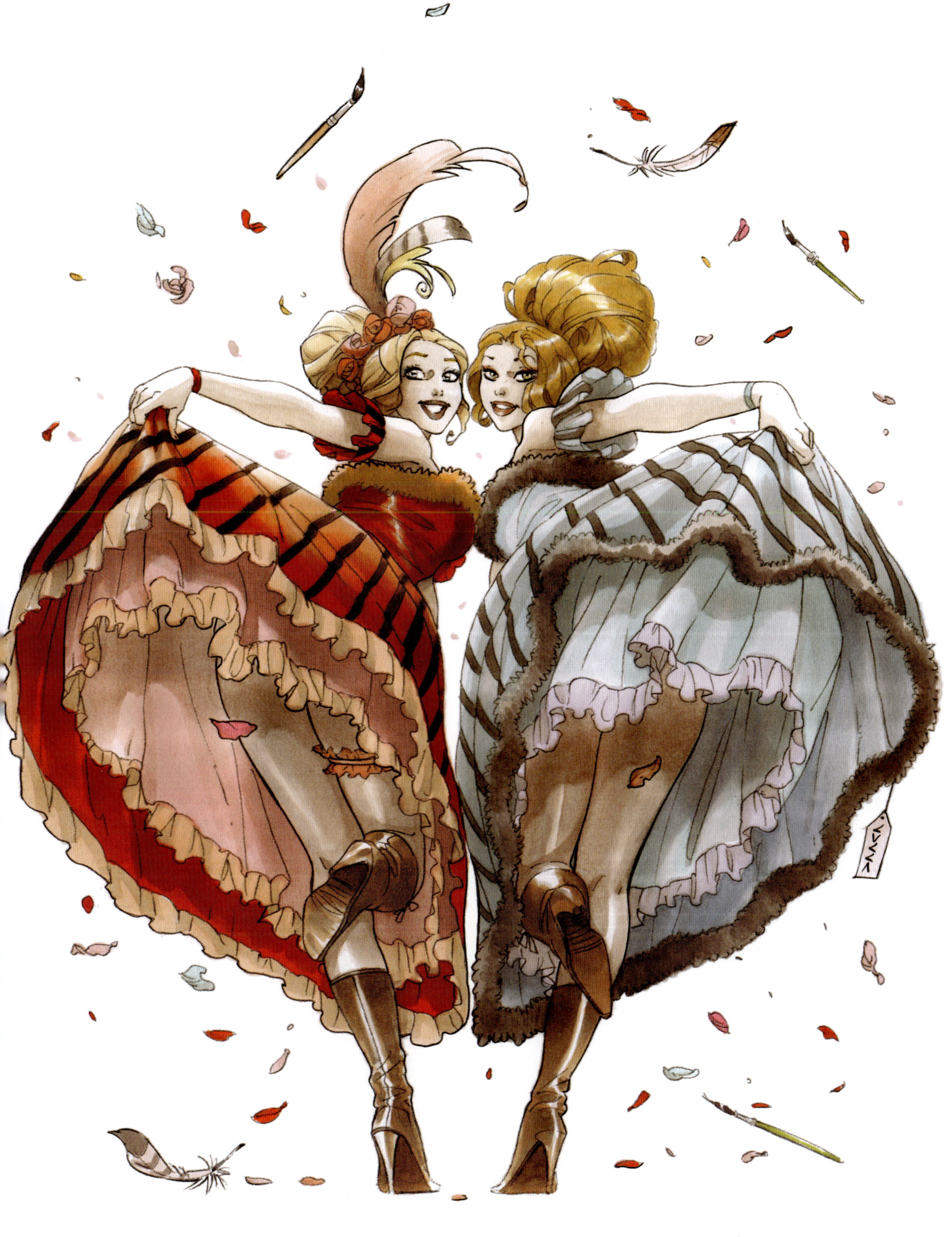

Can Can Can Do

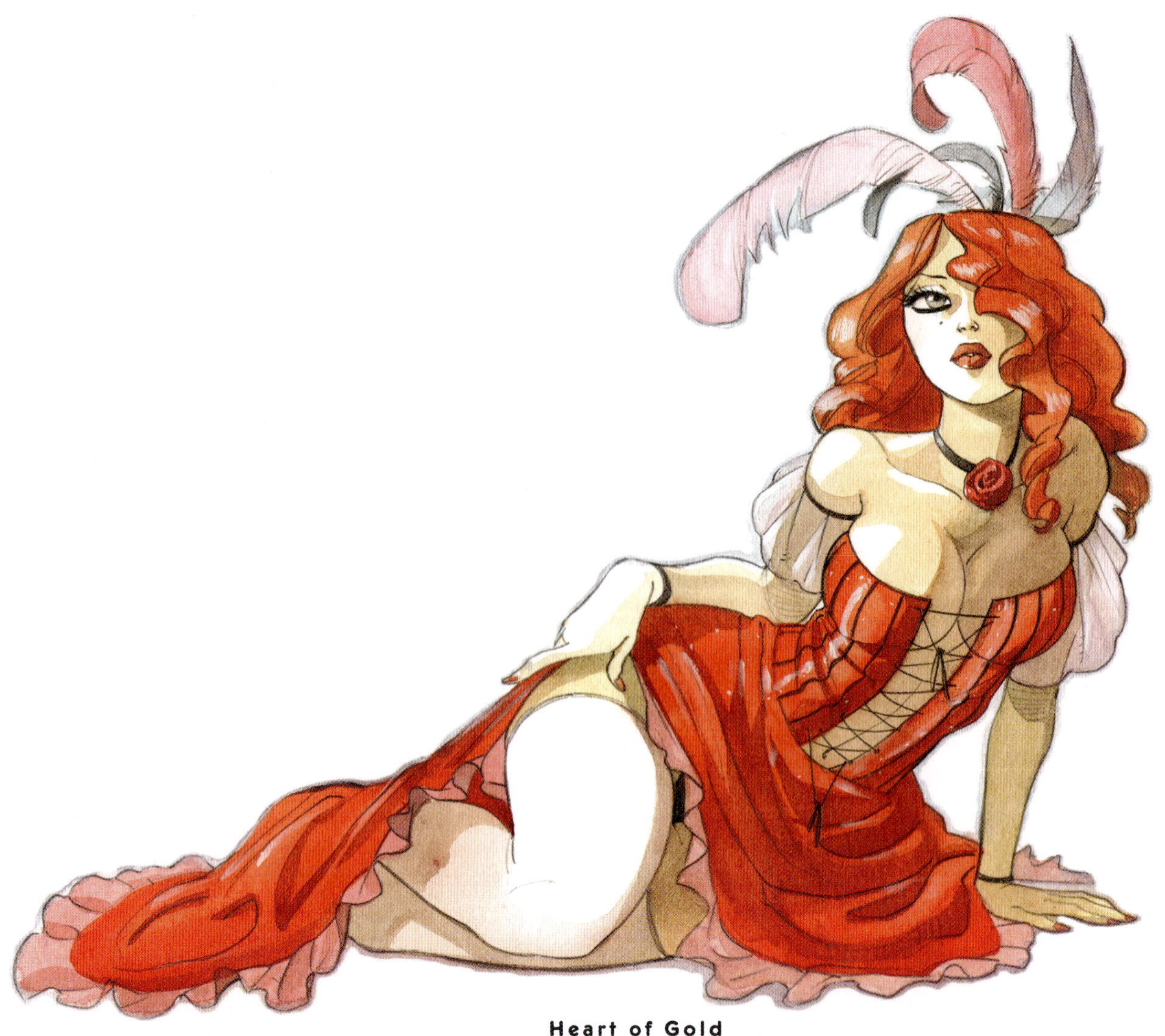

Heart of Gold

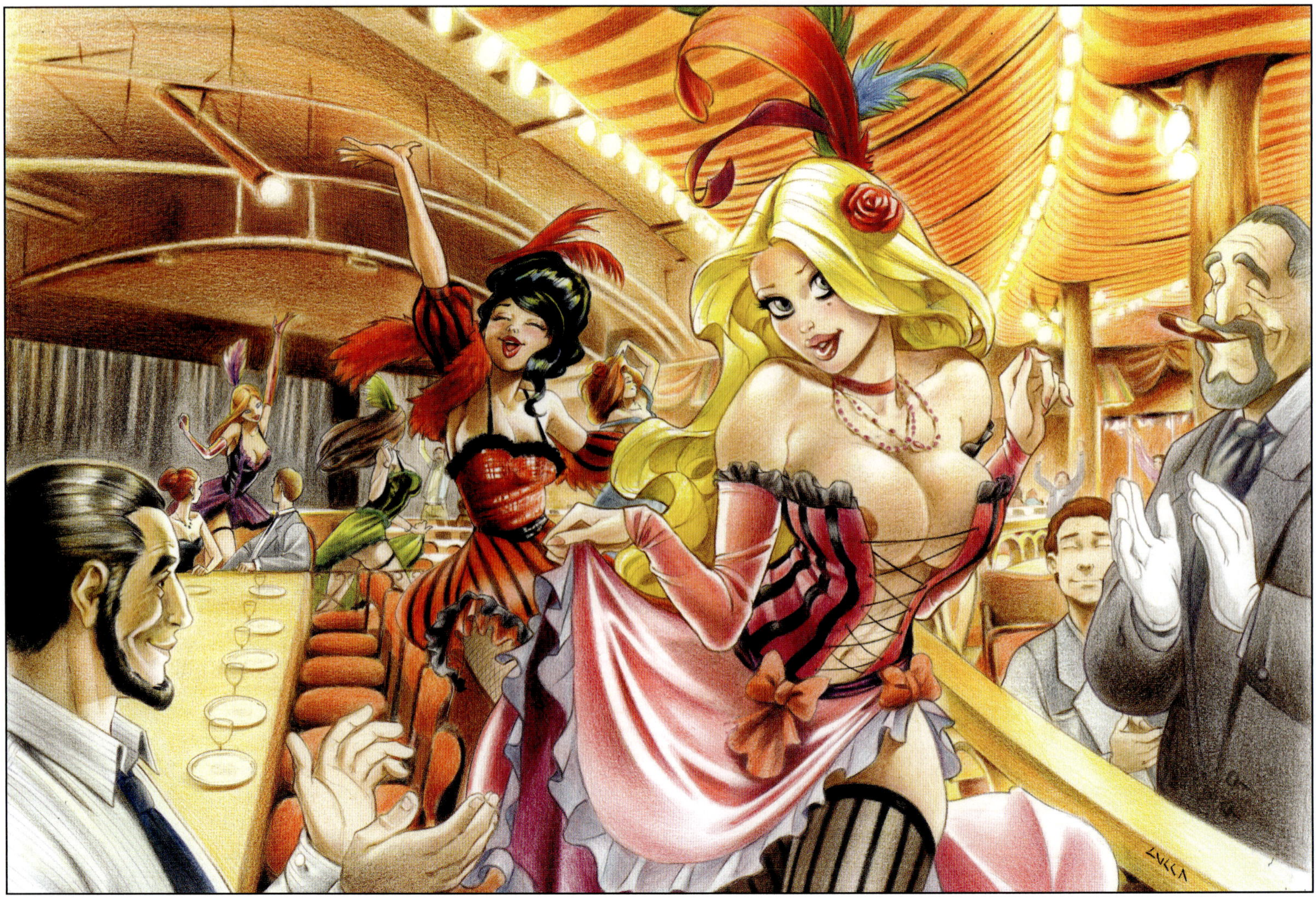

The Toast of Paris

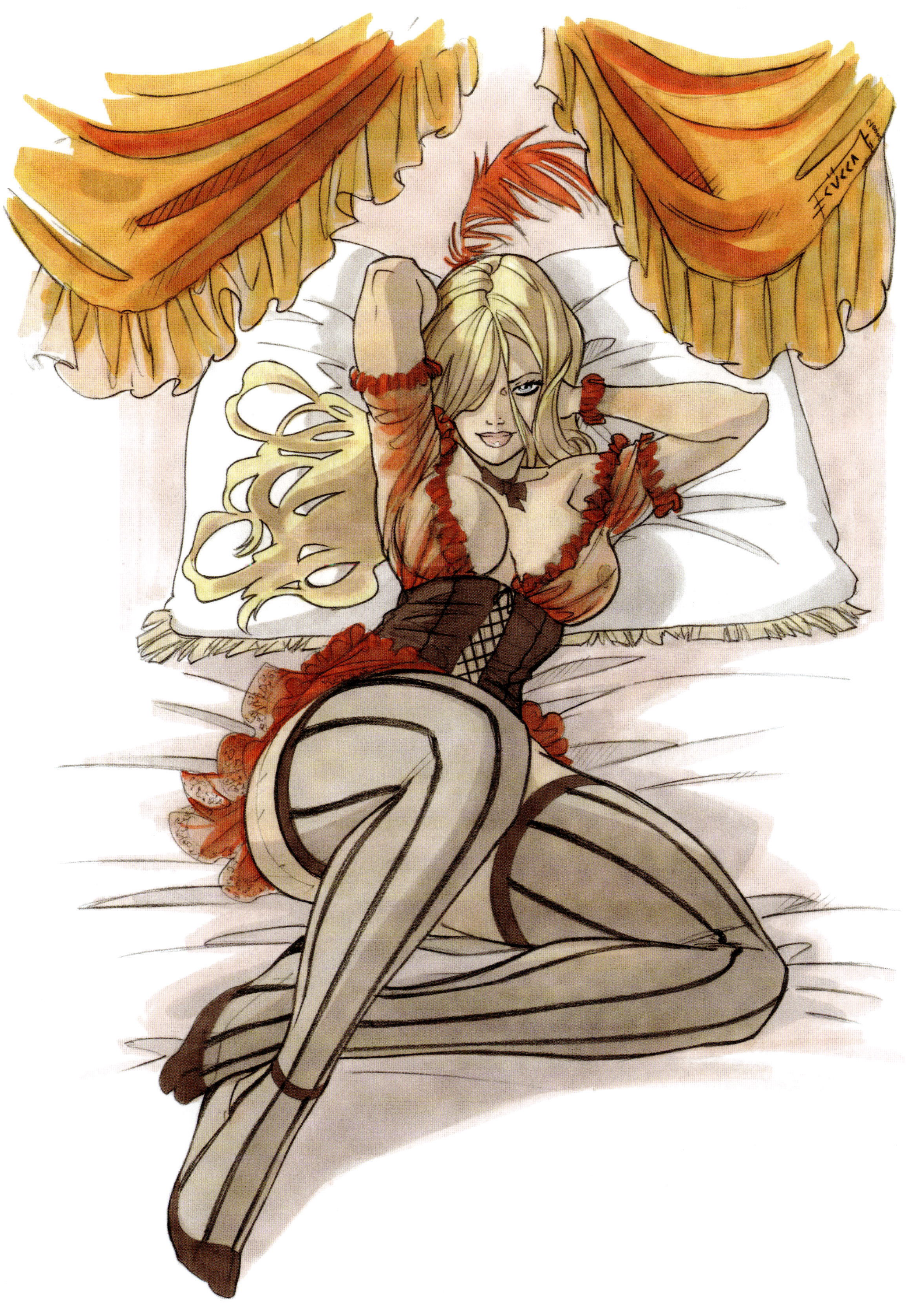

Wild West Pleasure

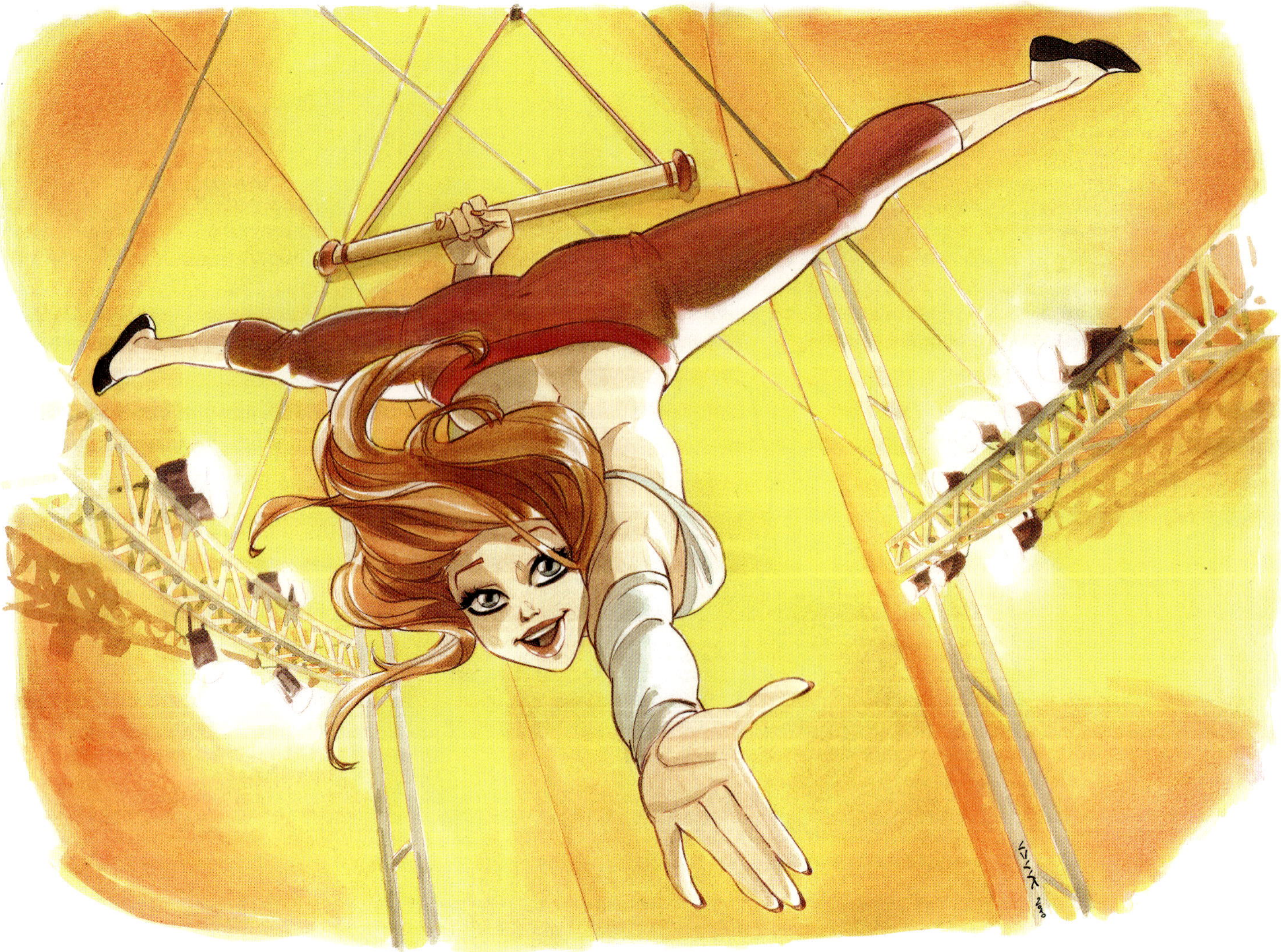

High Wire Act

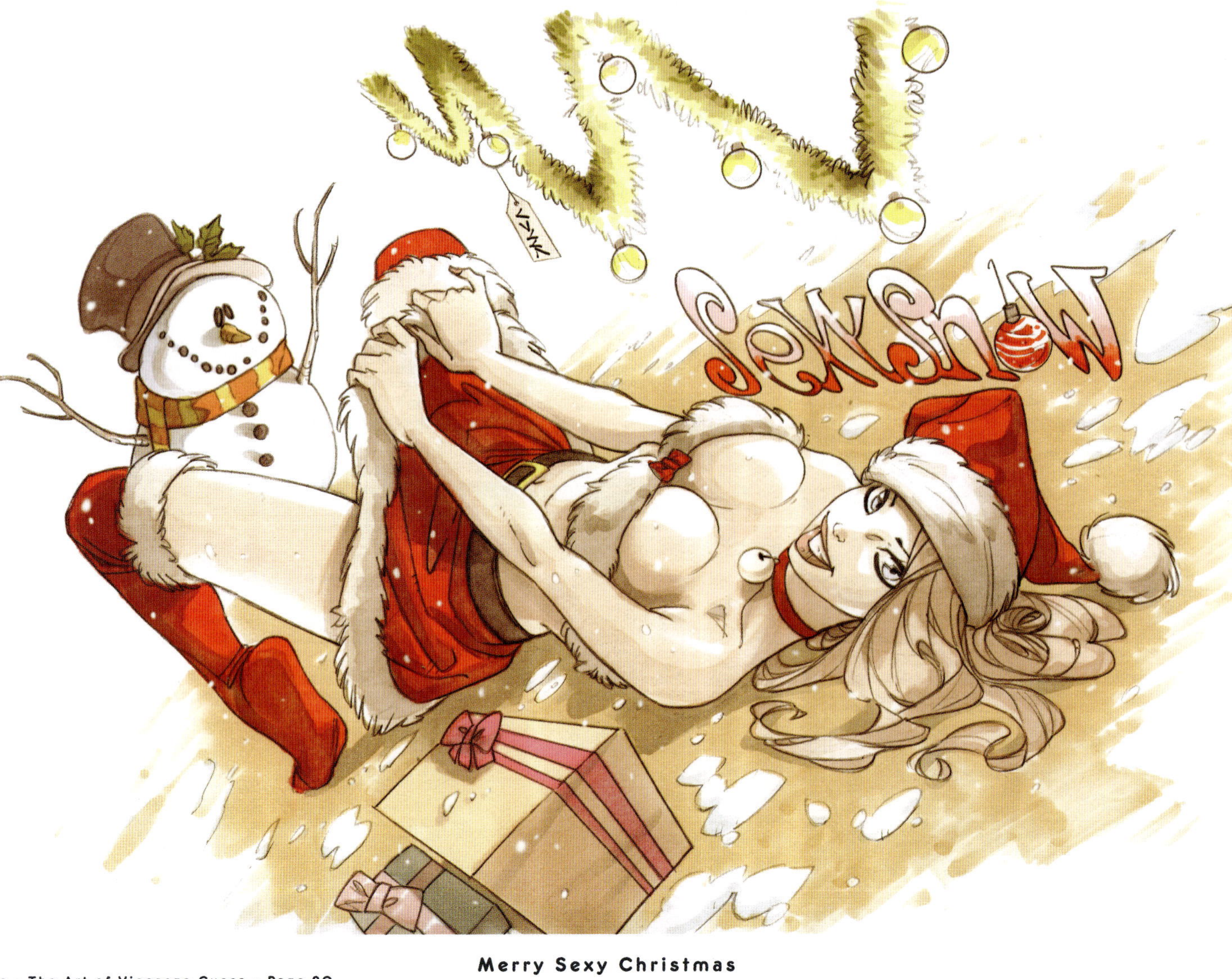

Merry Sexy Christmas

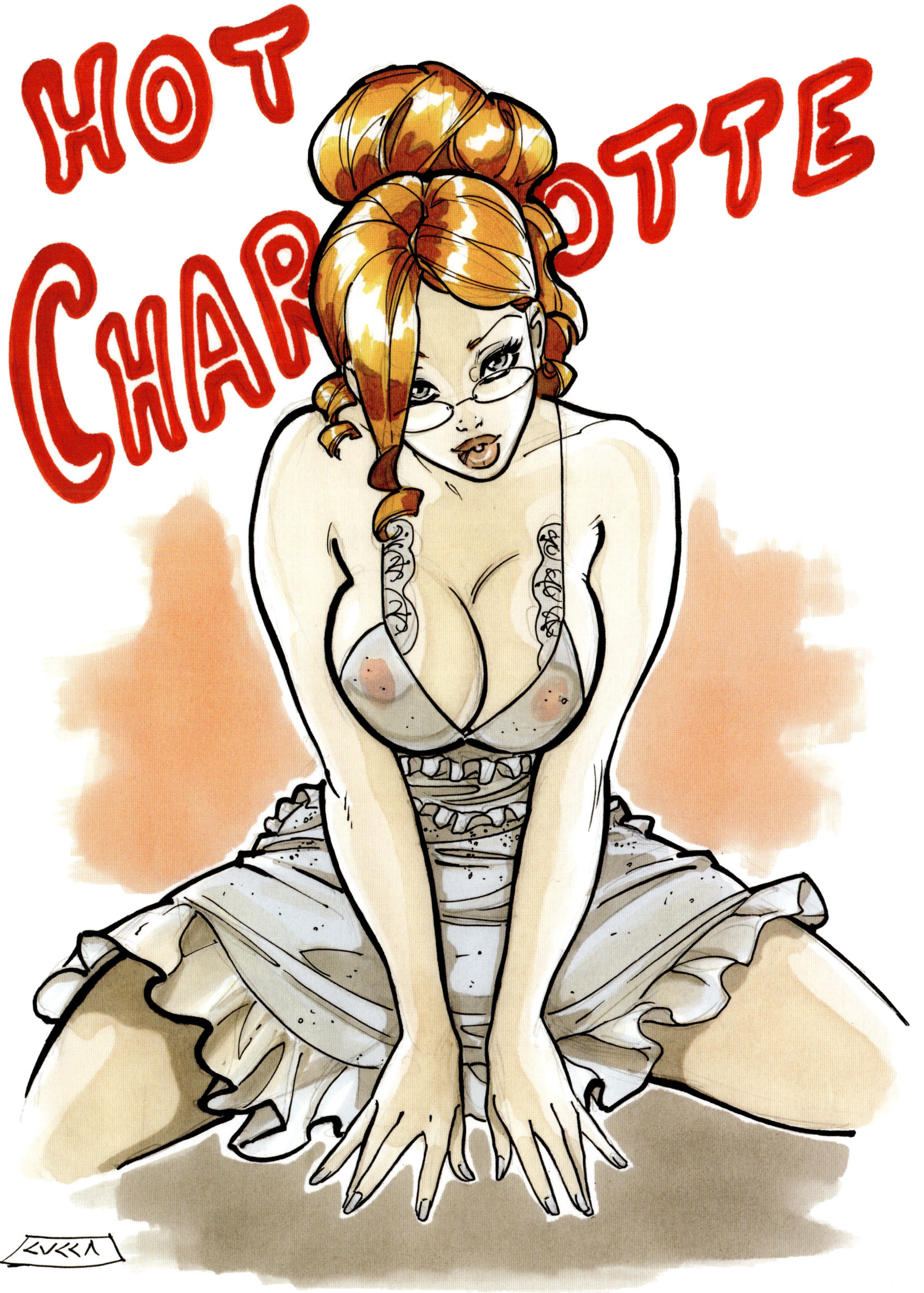

Hot Charlotte

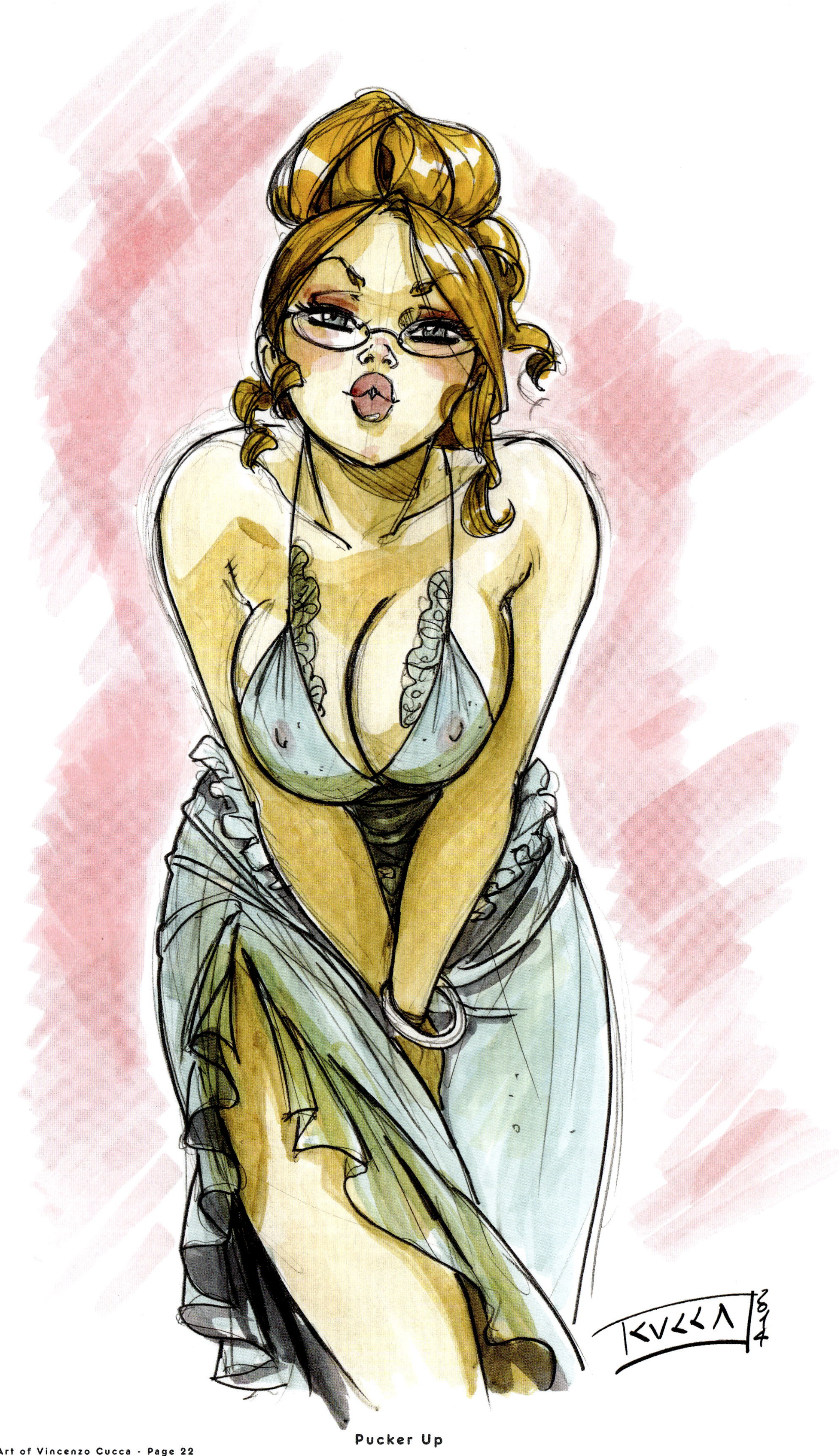

Pucker Up

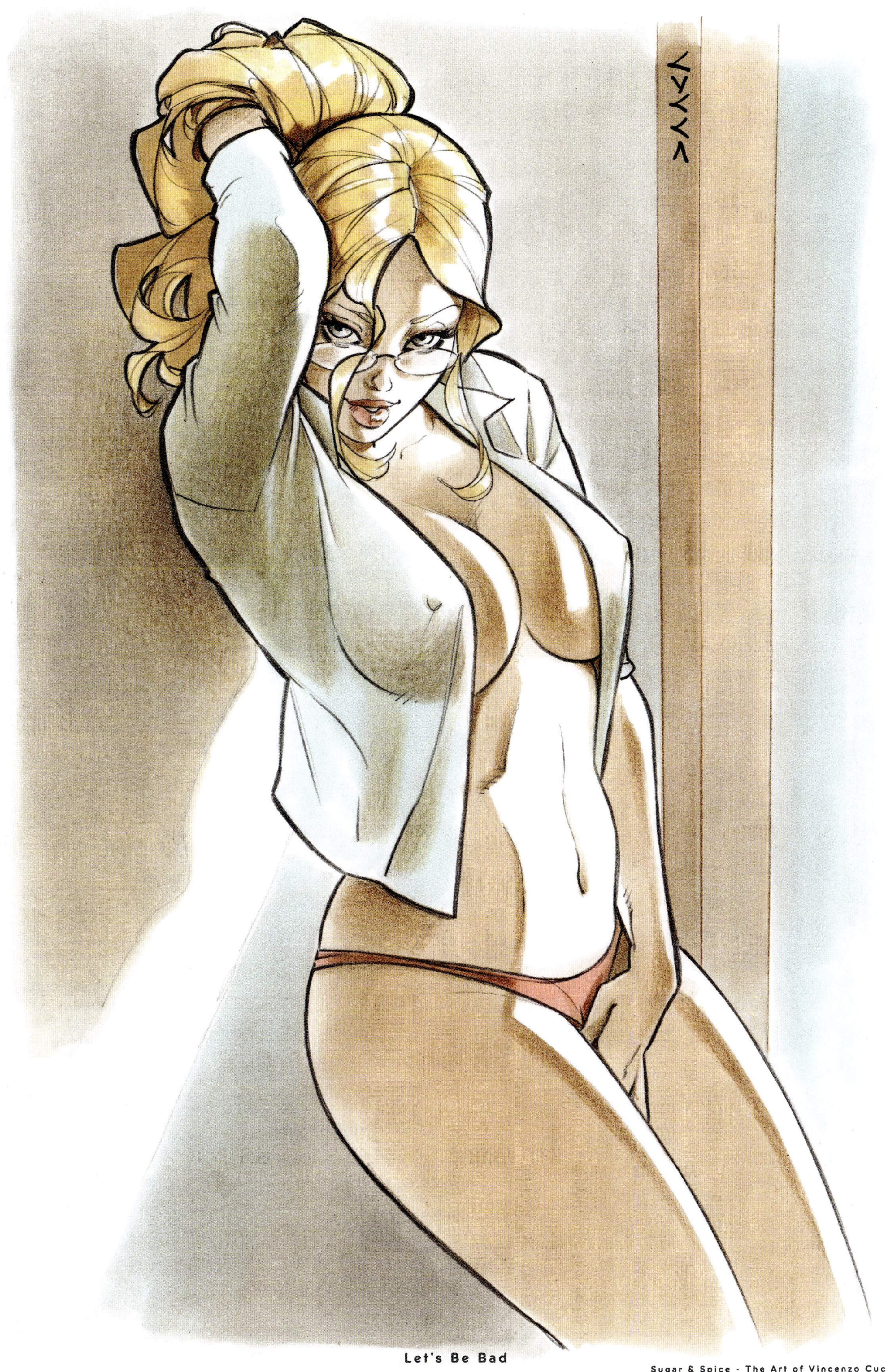

Let's Be Bad

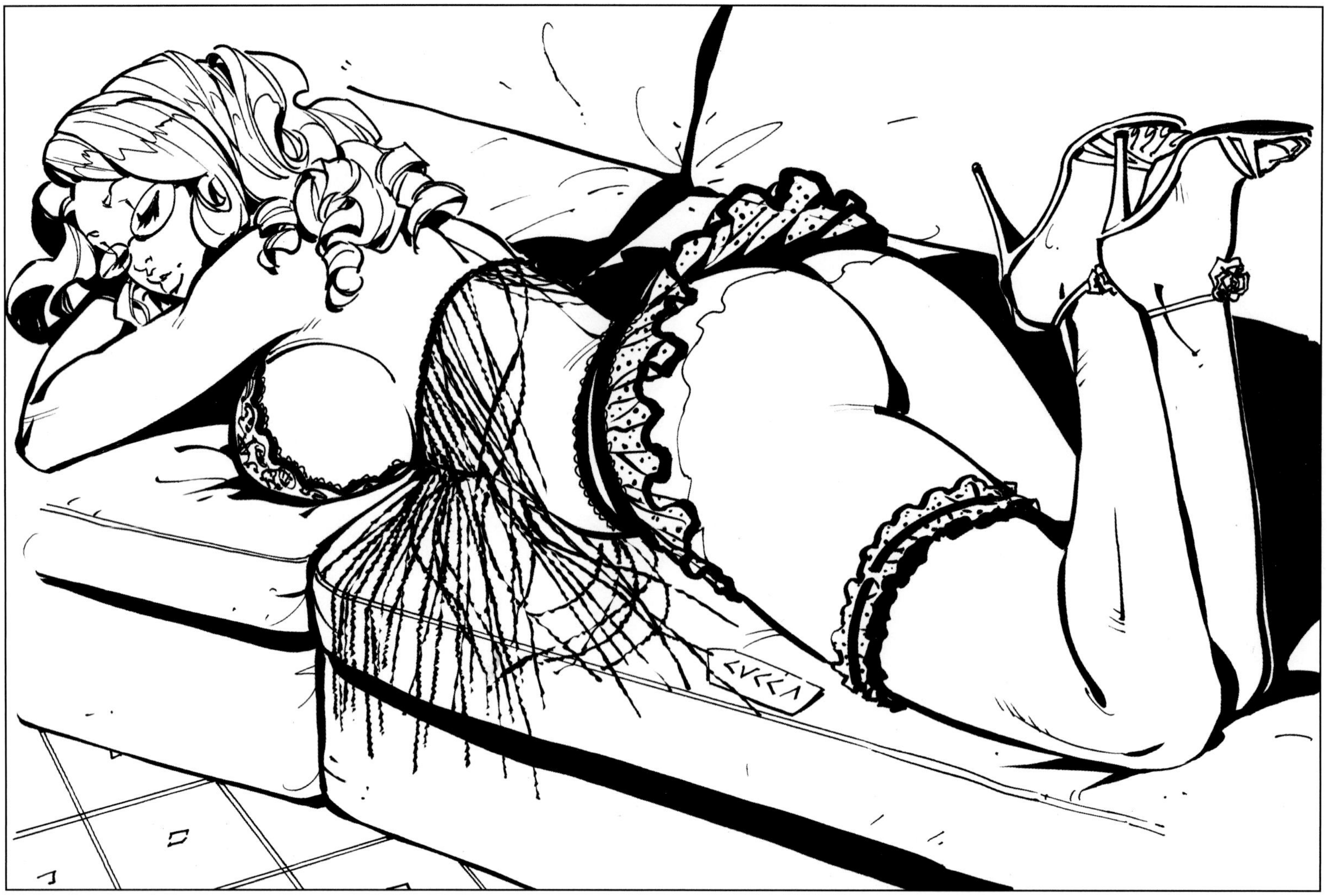

This End Up

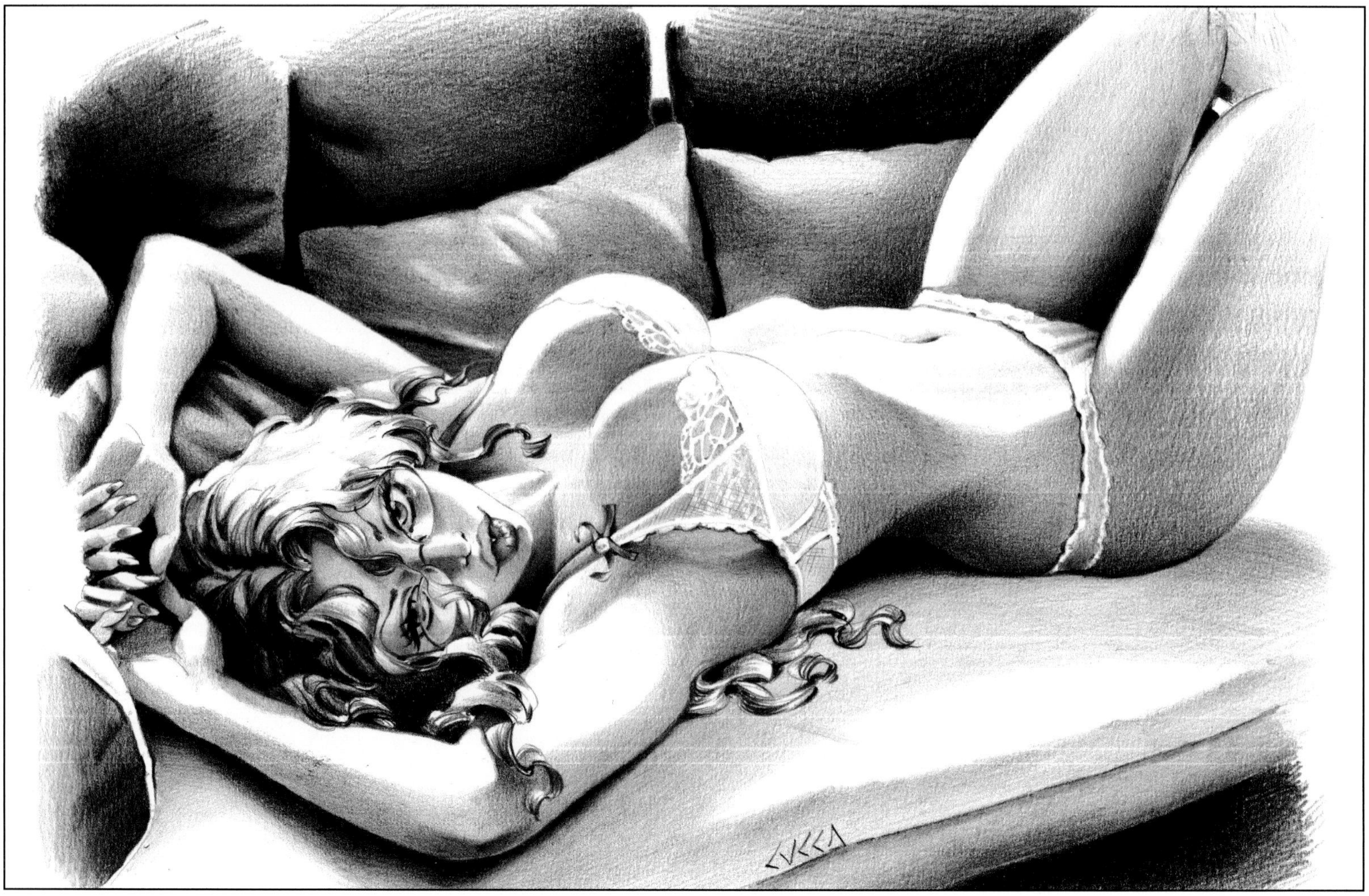

Smoulder

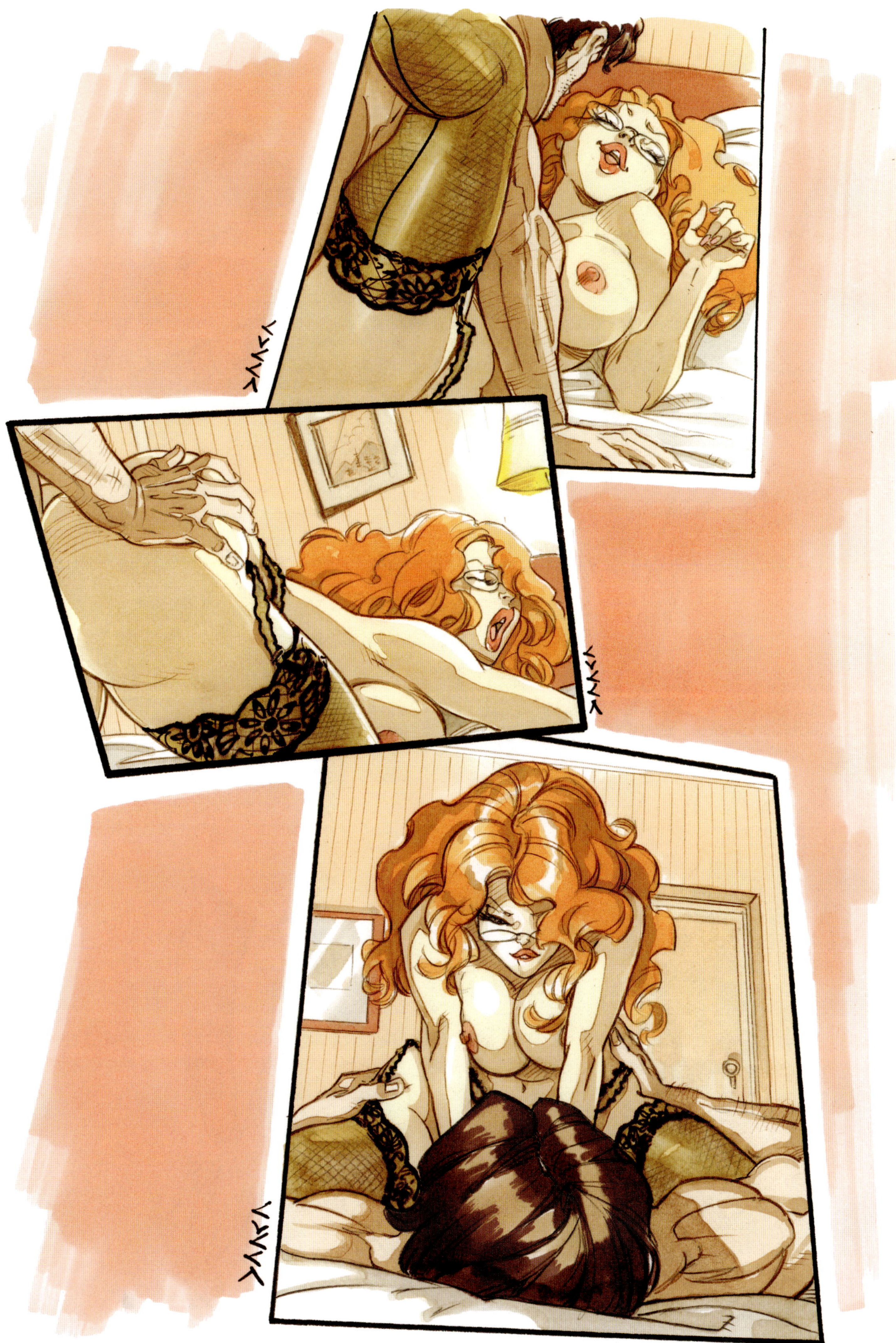

Triple Play

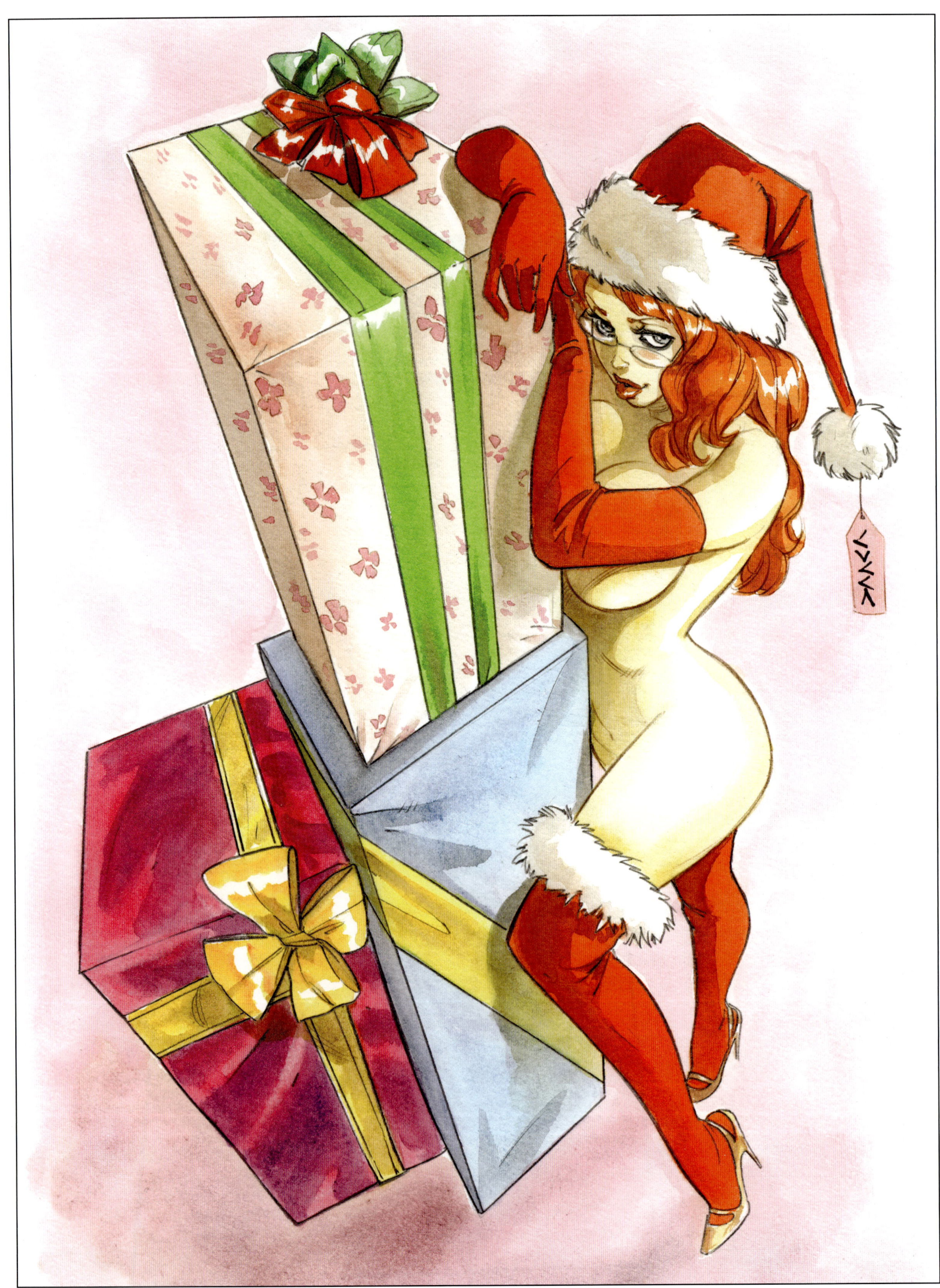

She KNOWS When You've Been Naughty

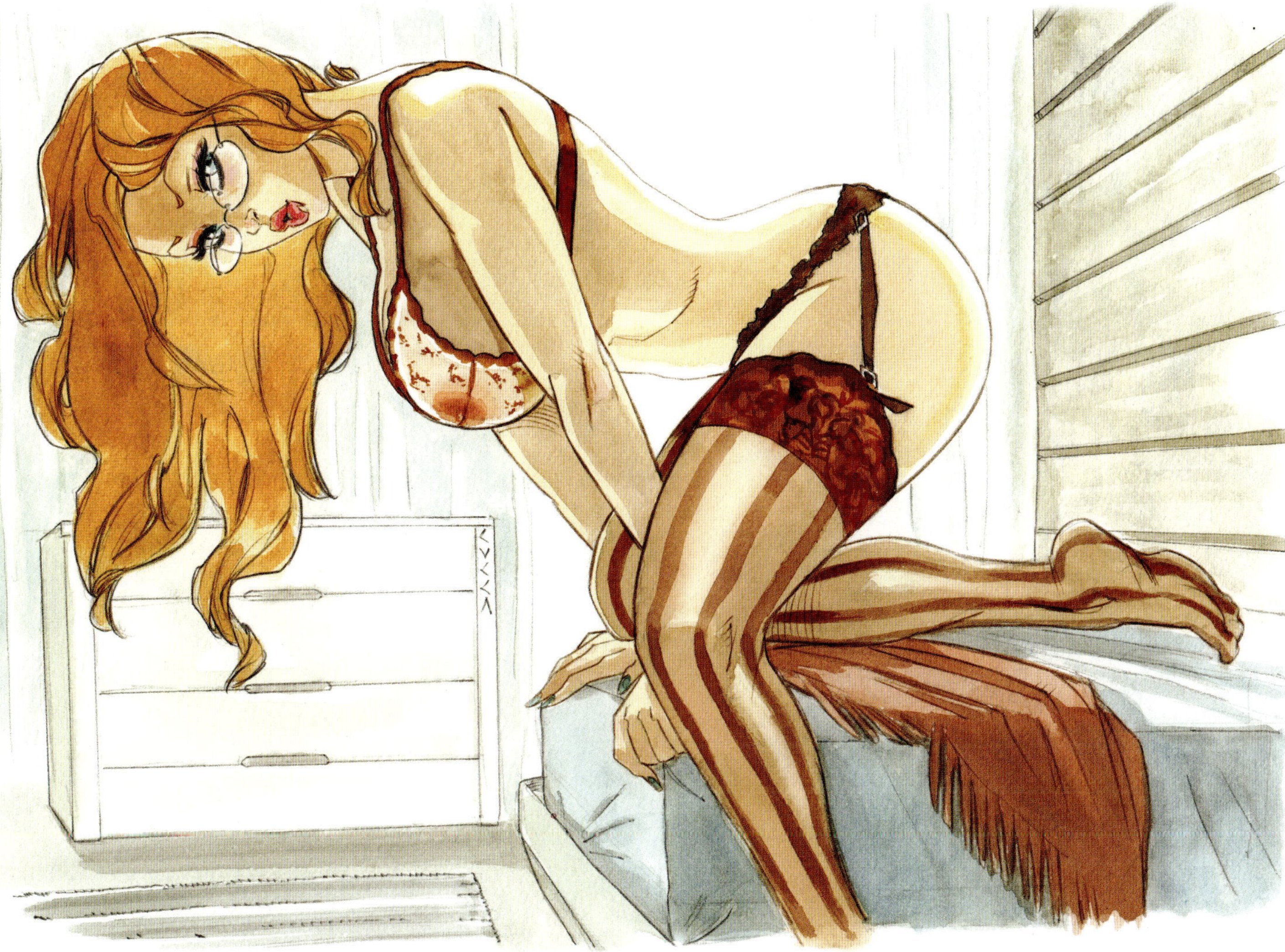

Anticipation

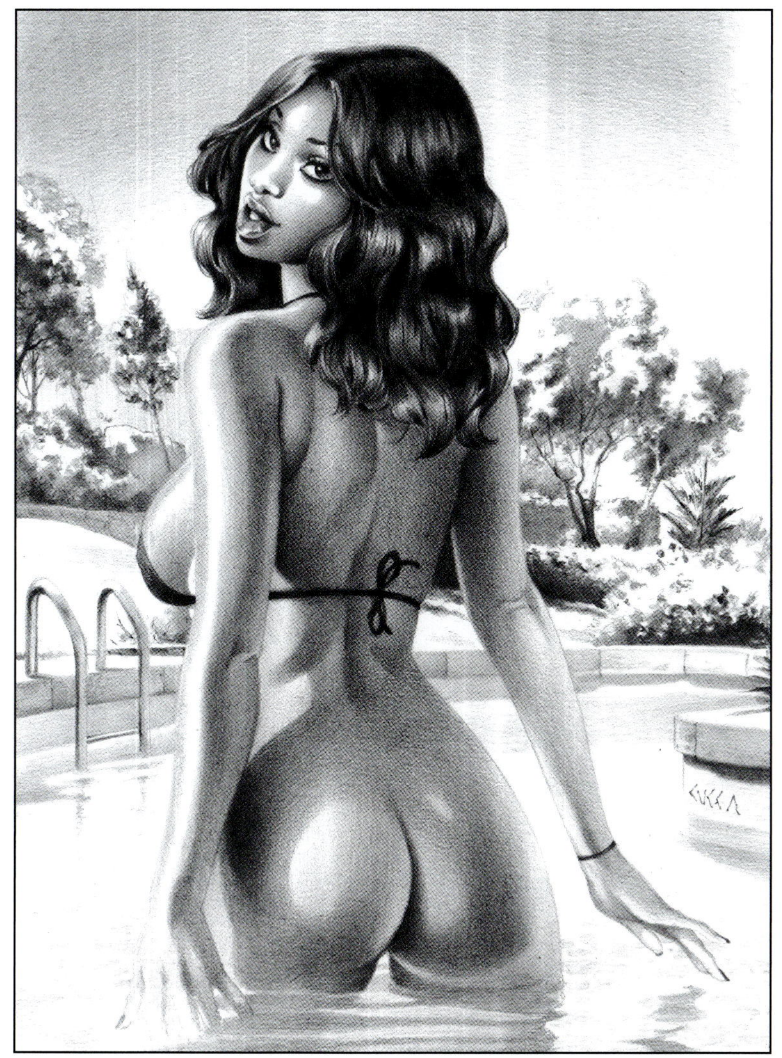

Aline

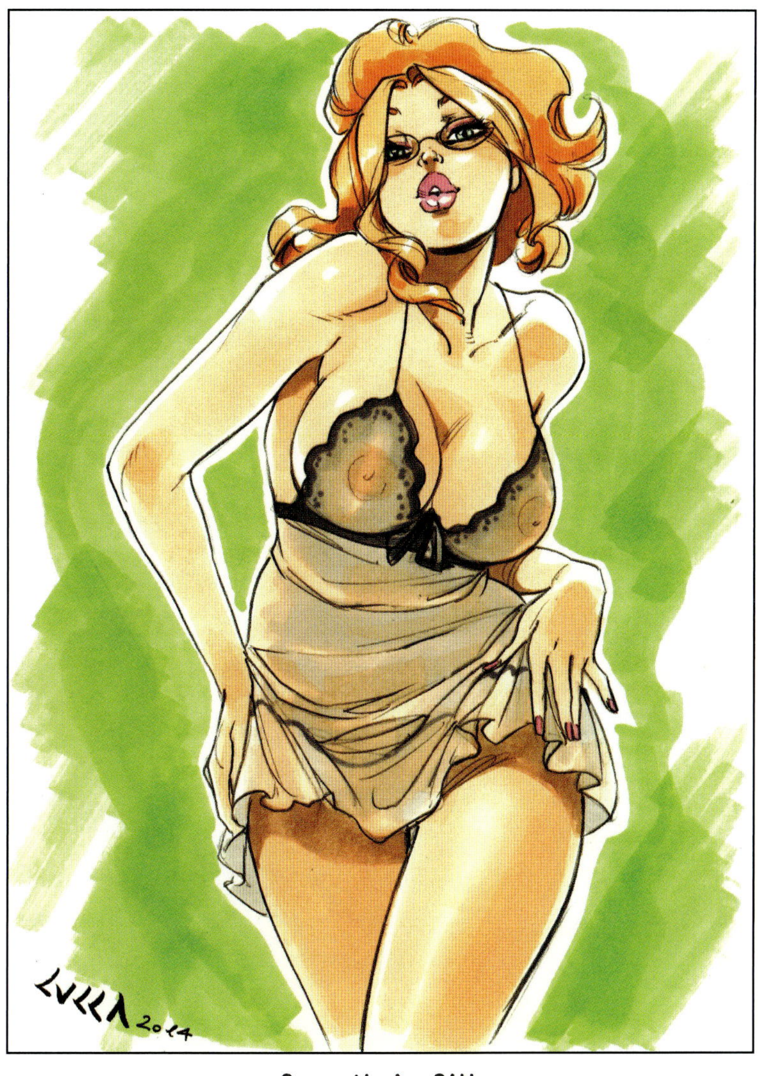

Smooth As Silk

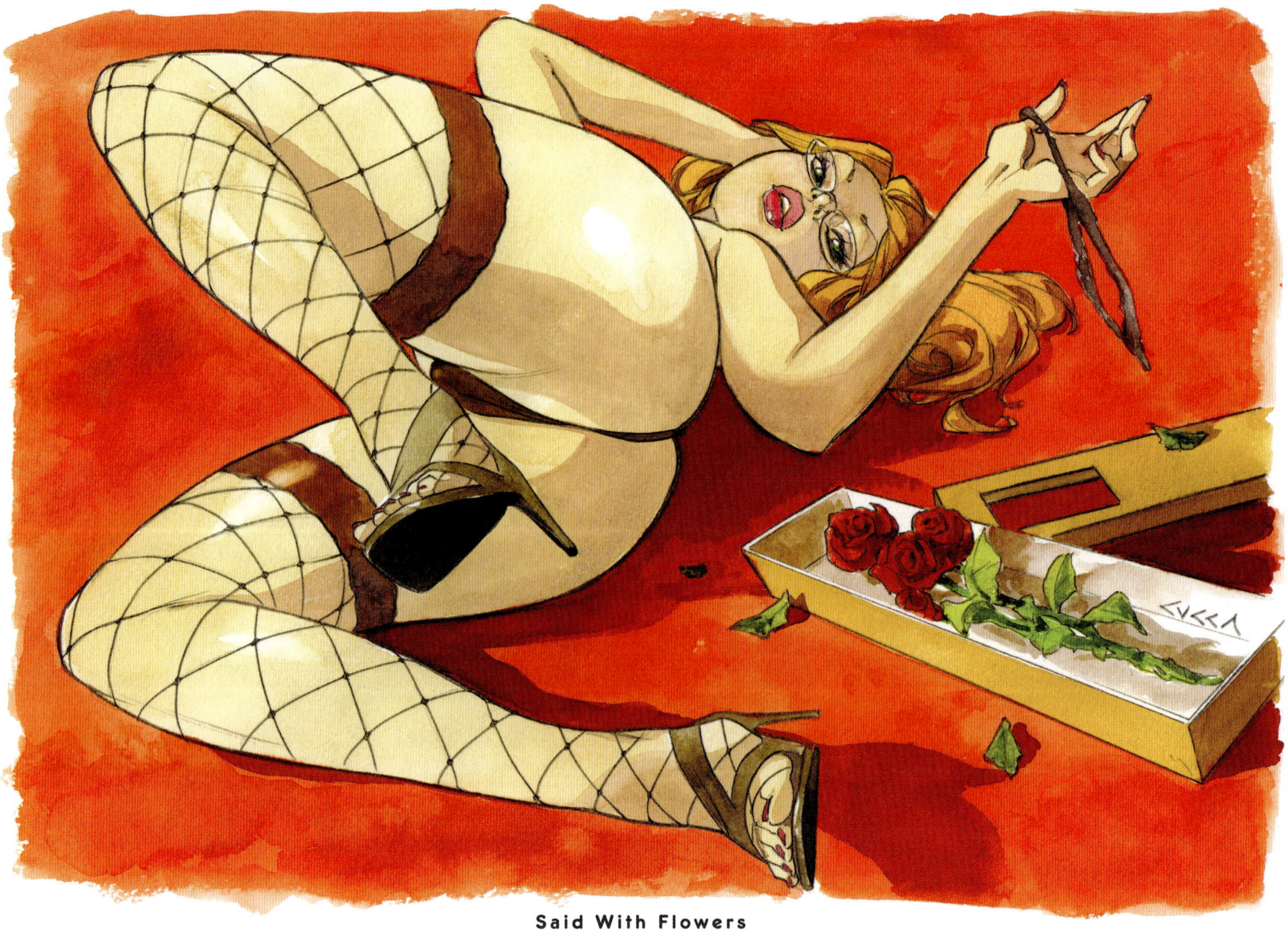

Said With Flowers

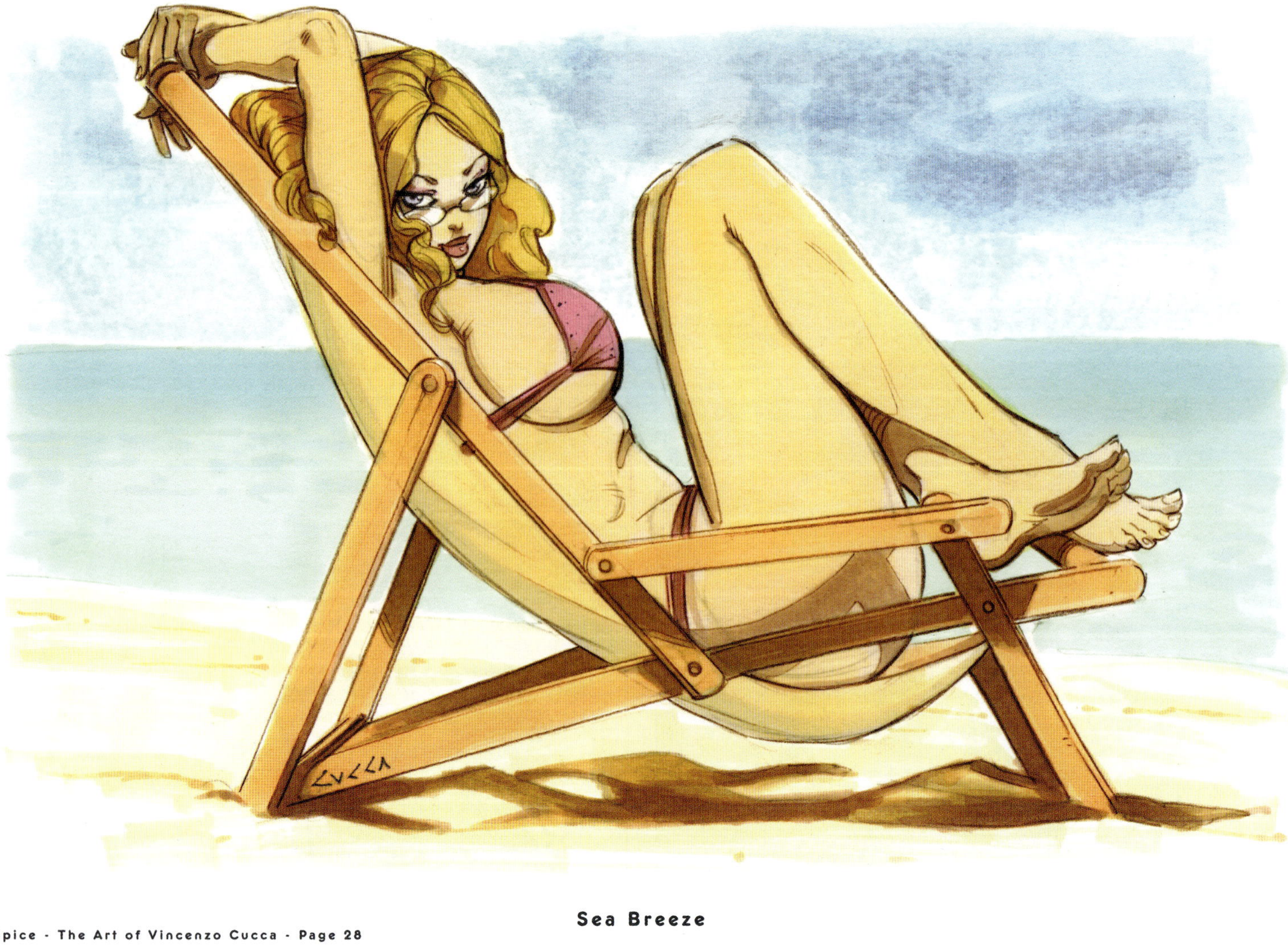

Sea Breeze

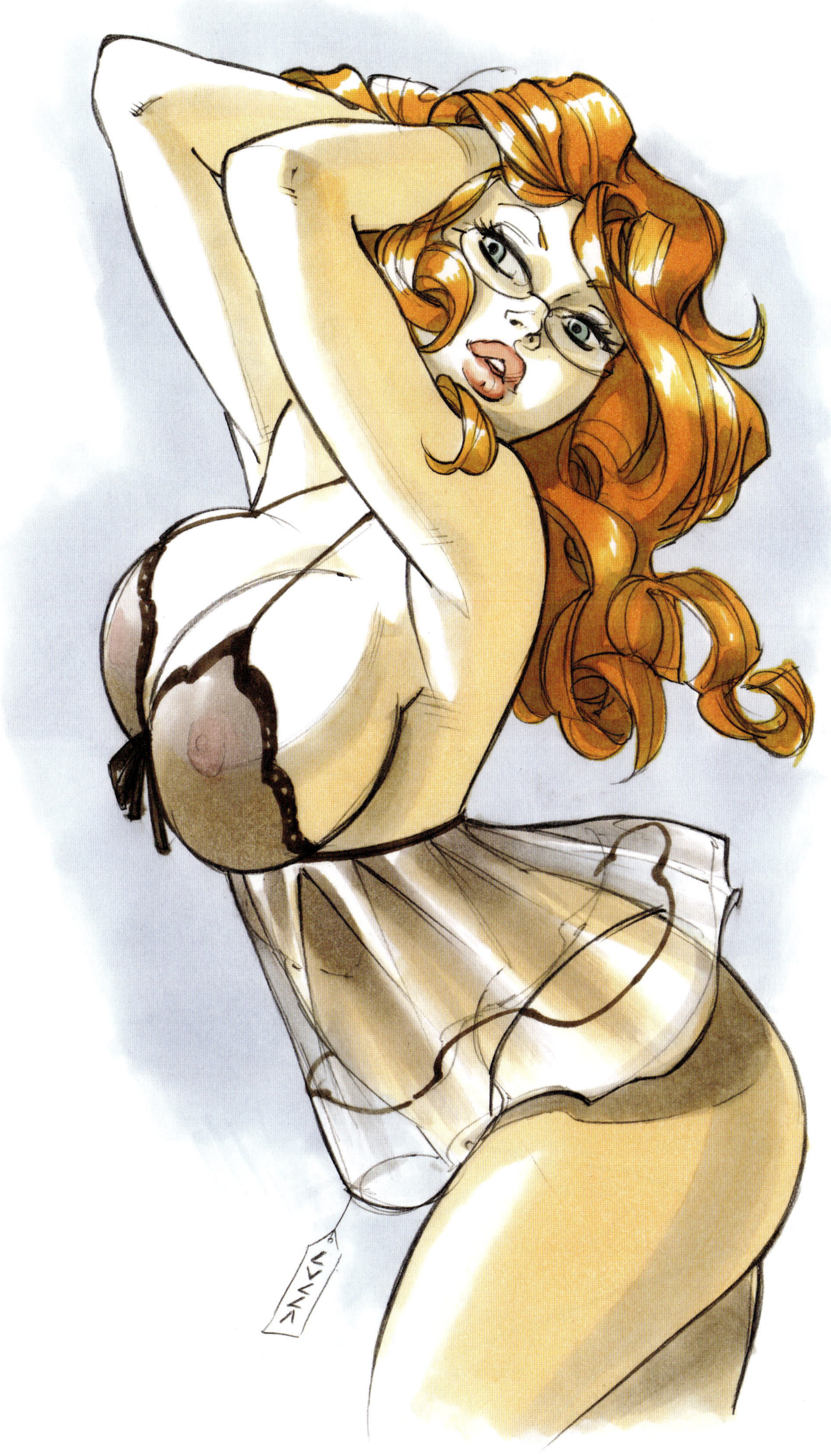

Flimsy Excuse

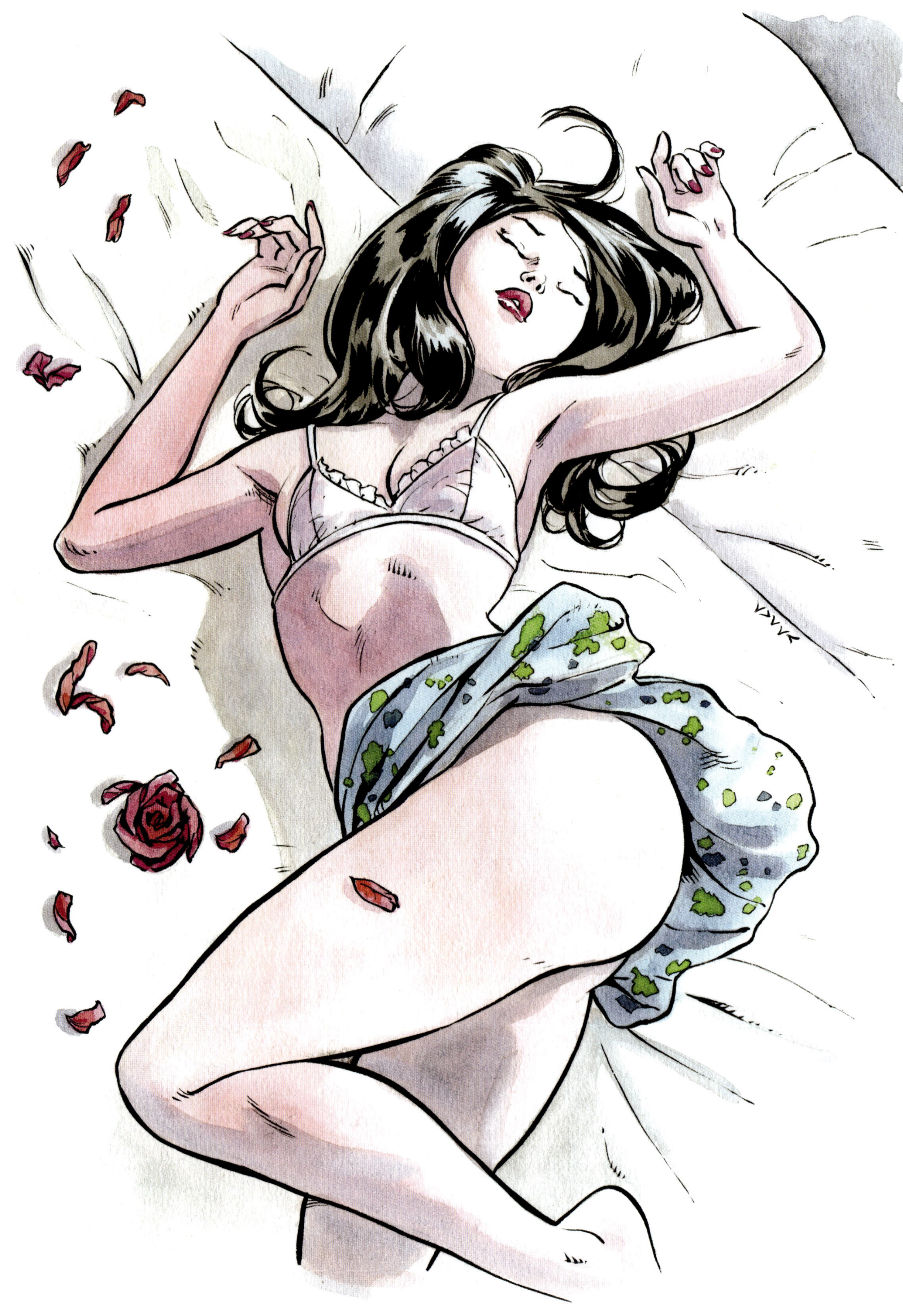

Sweet Dreams

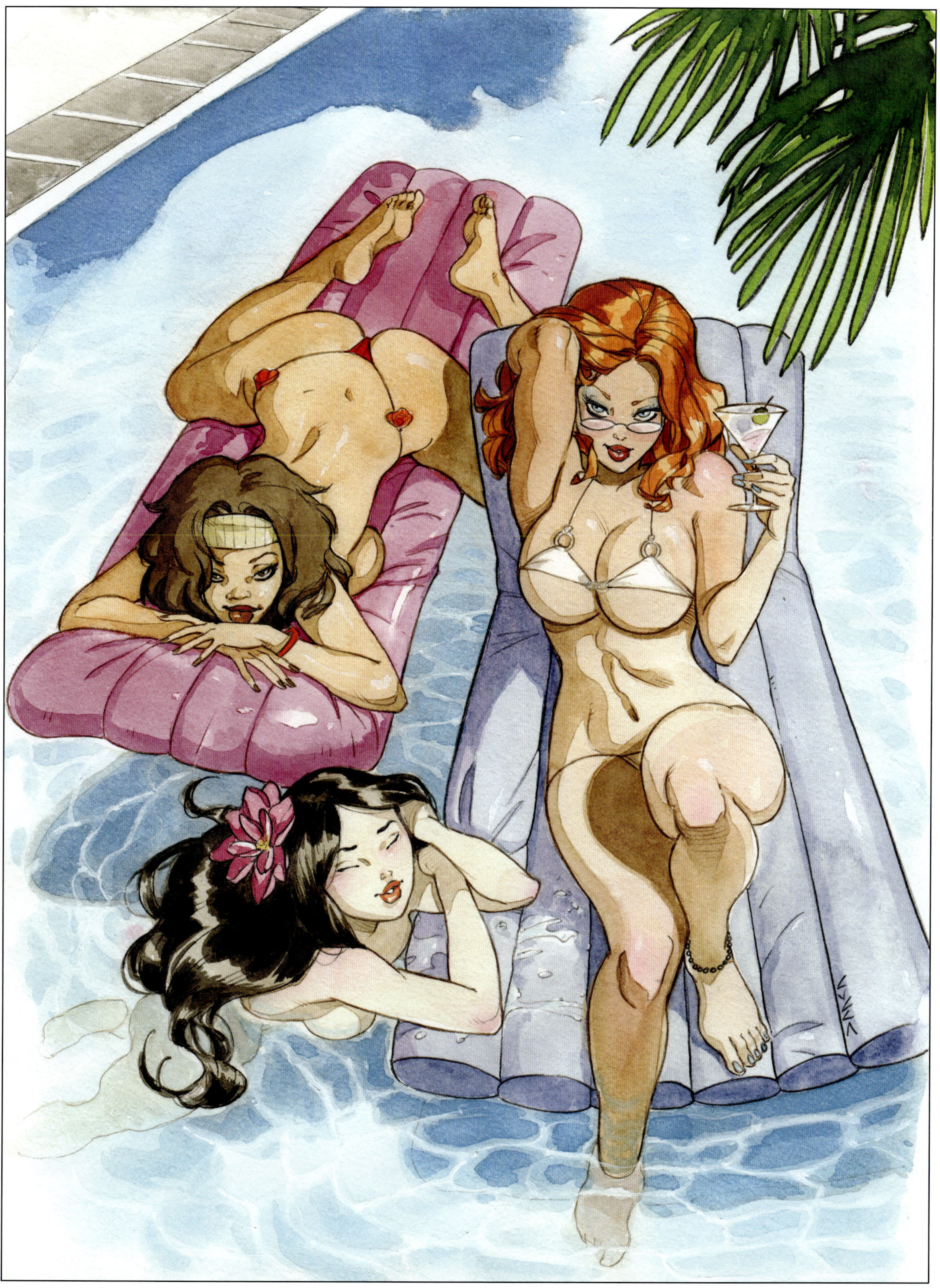

Poolside Sirens

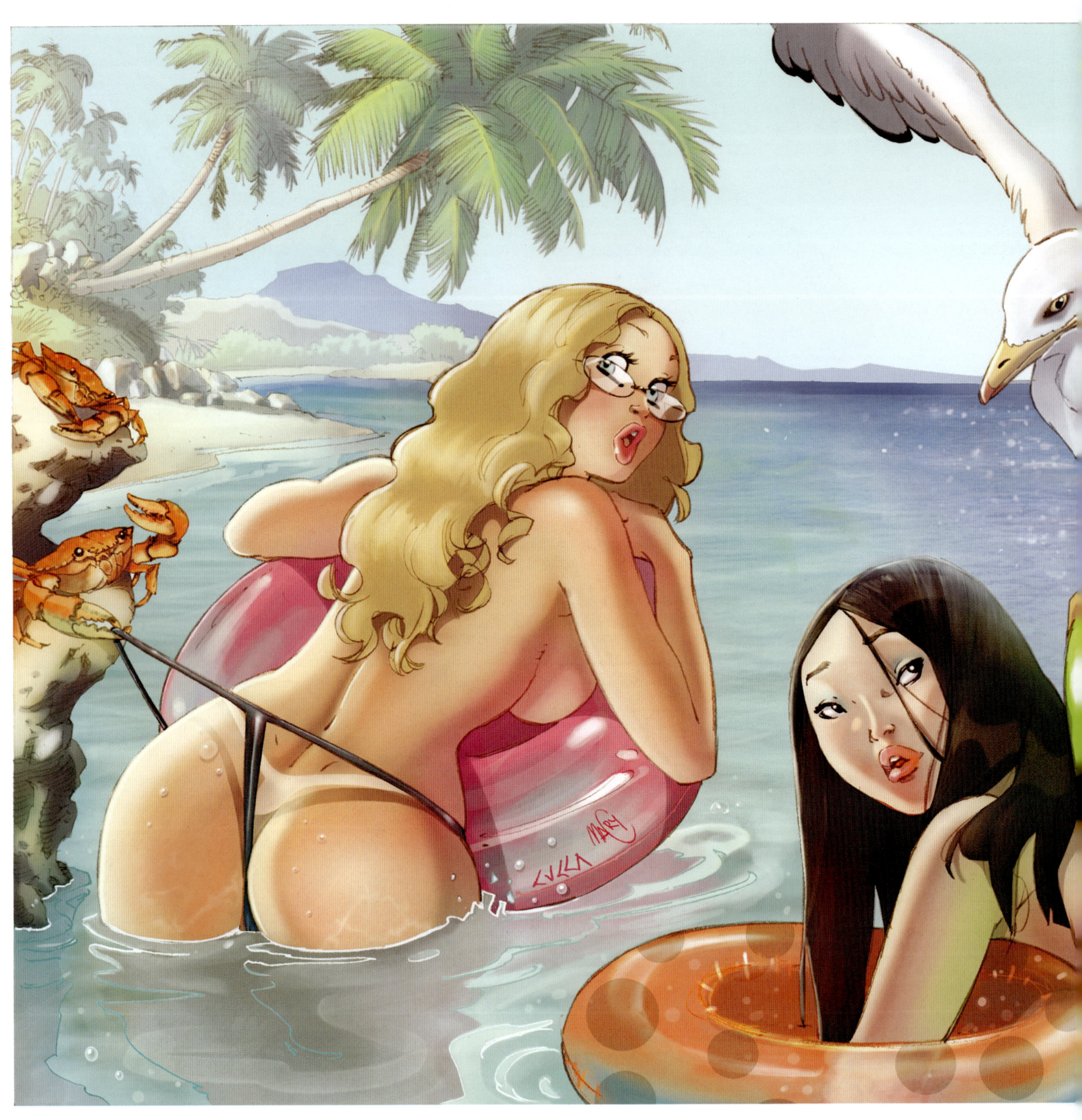

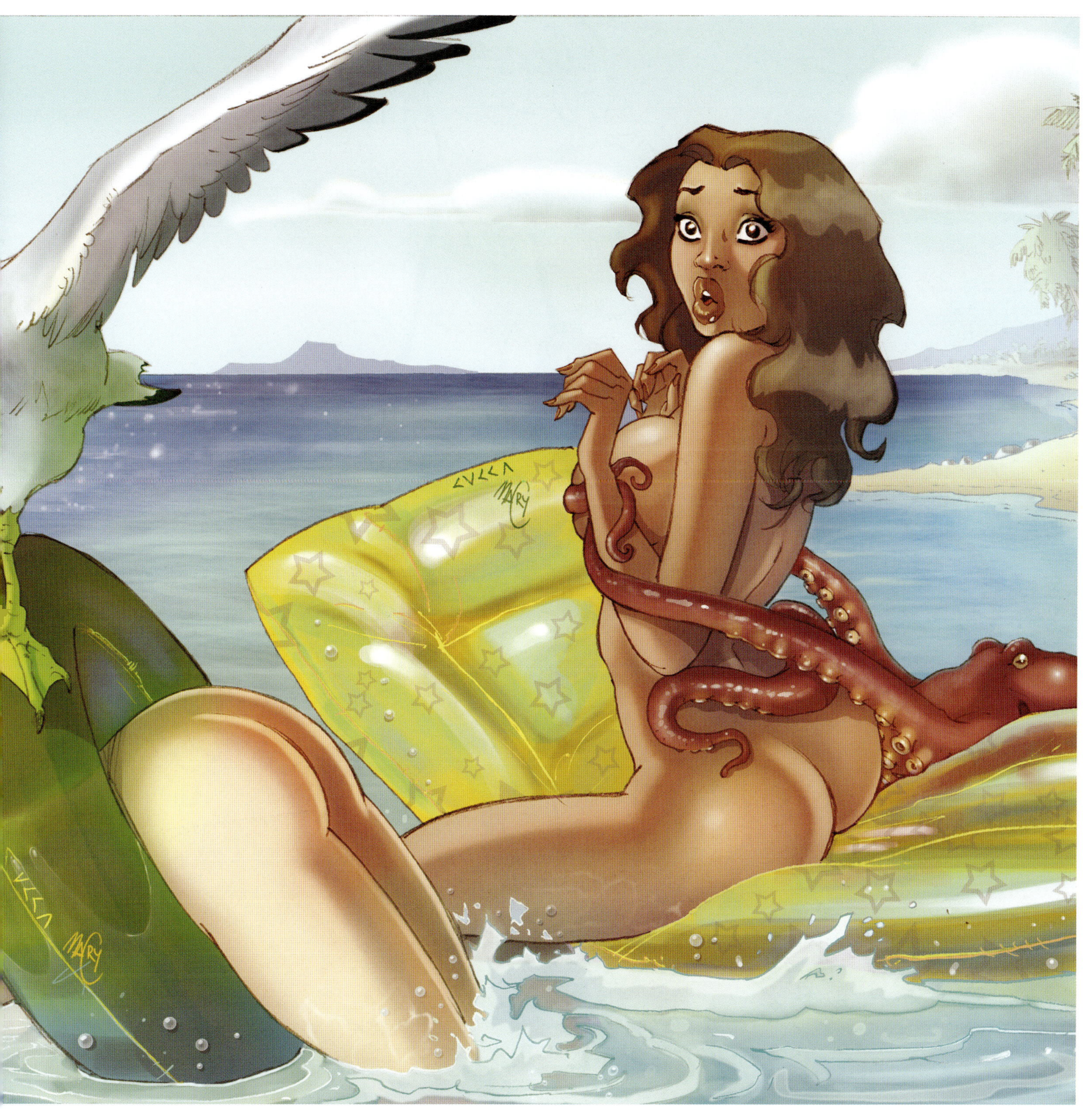

Fun In The Sun (color by Mariacristina Federico)

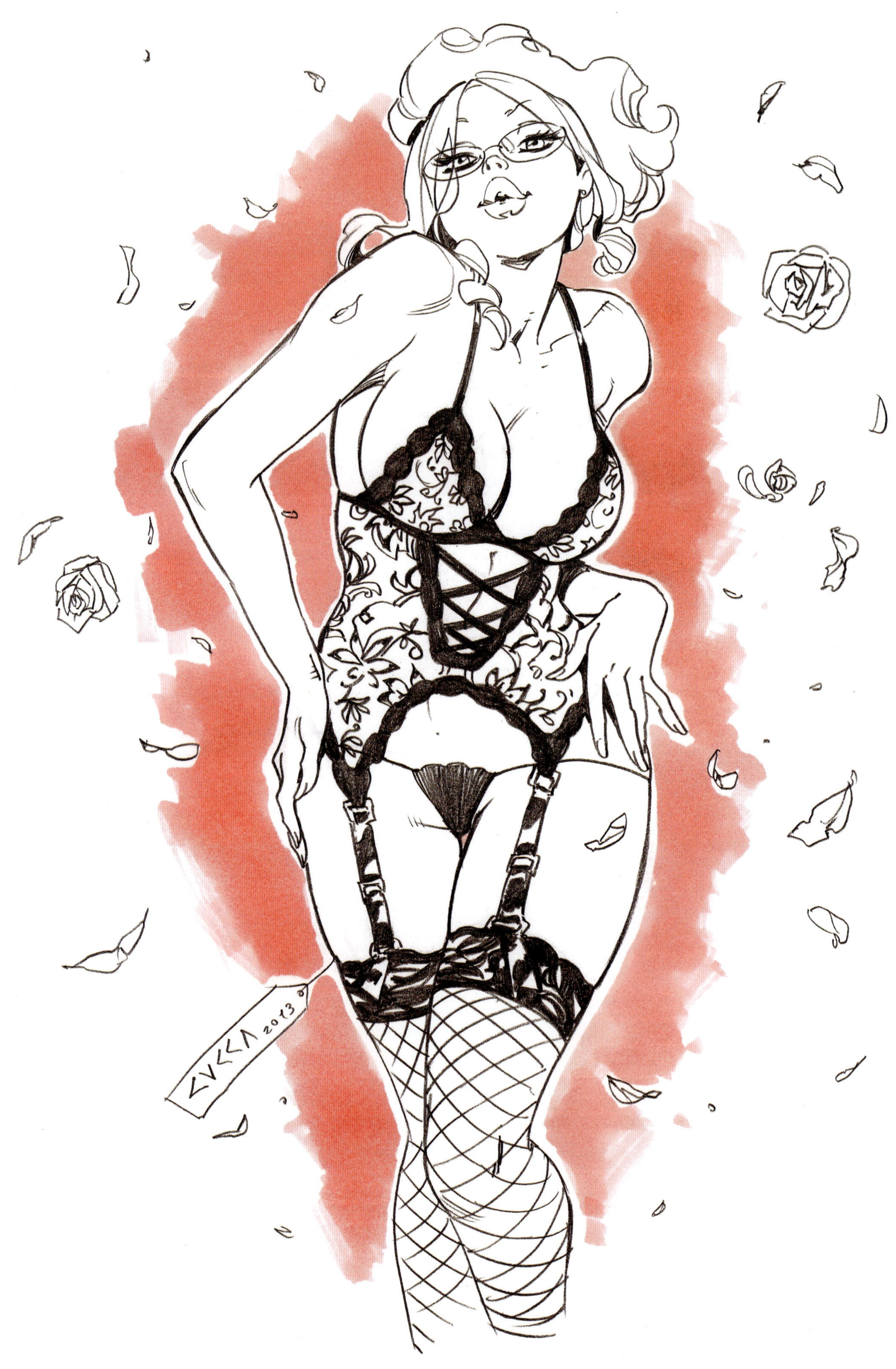

Panty Parade

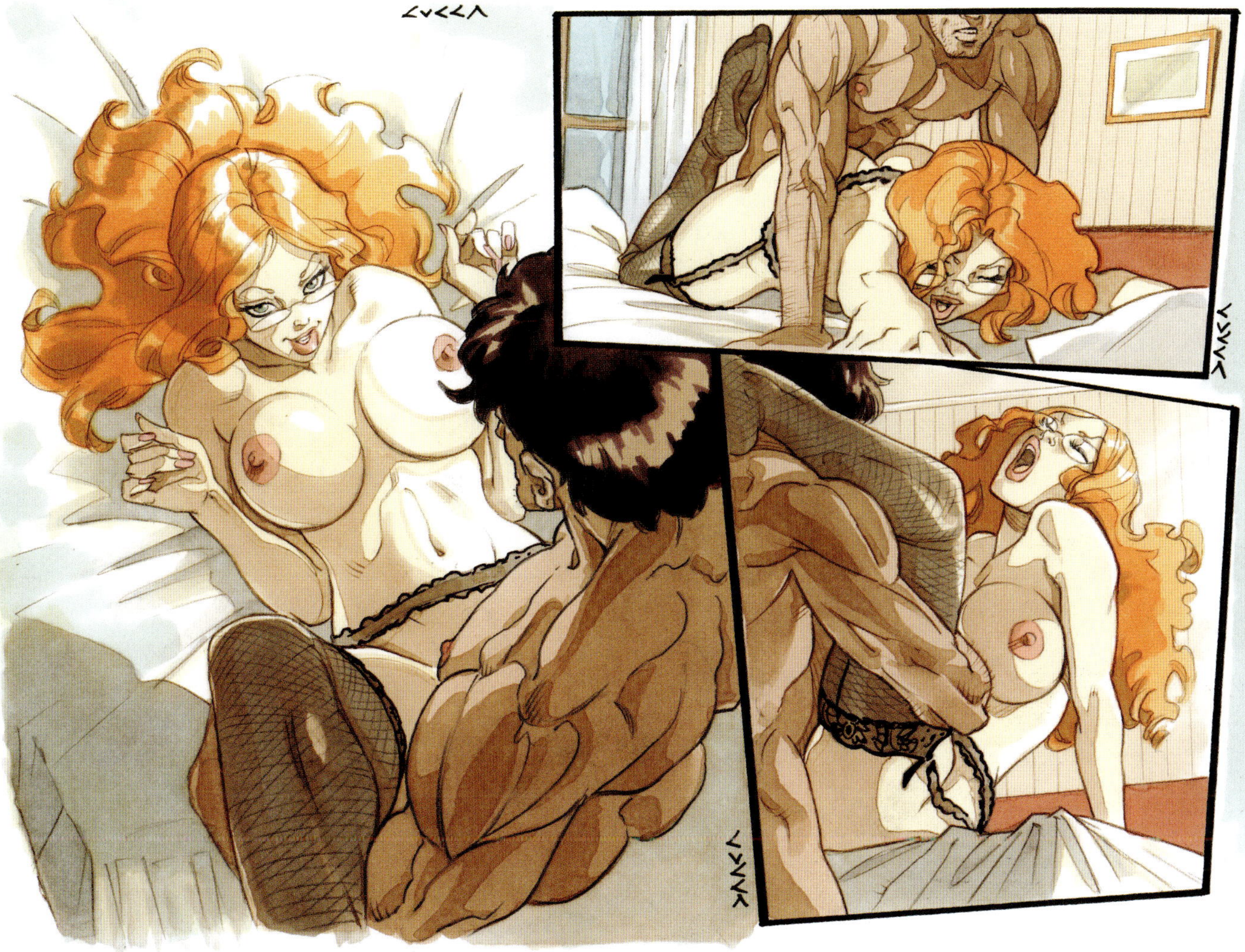

A Night To Remember

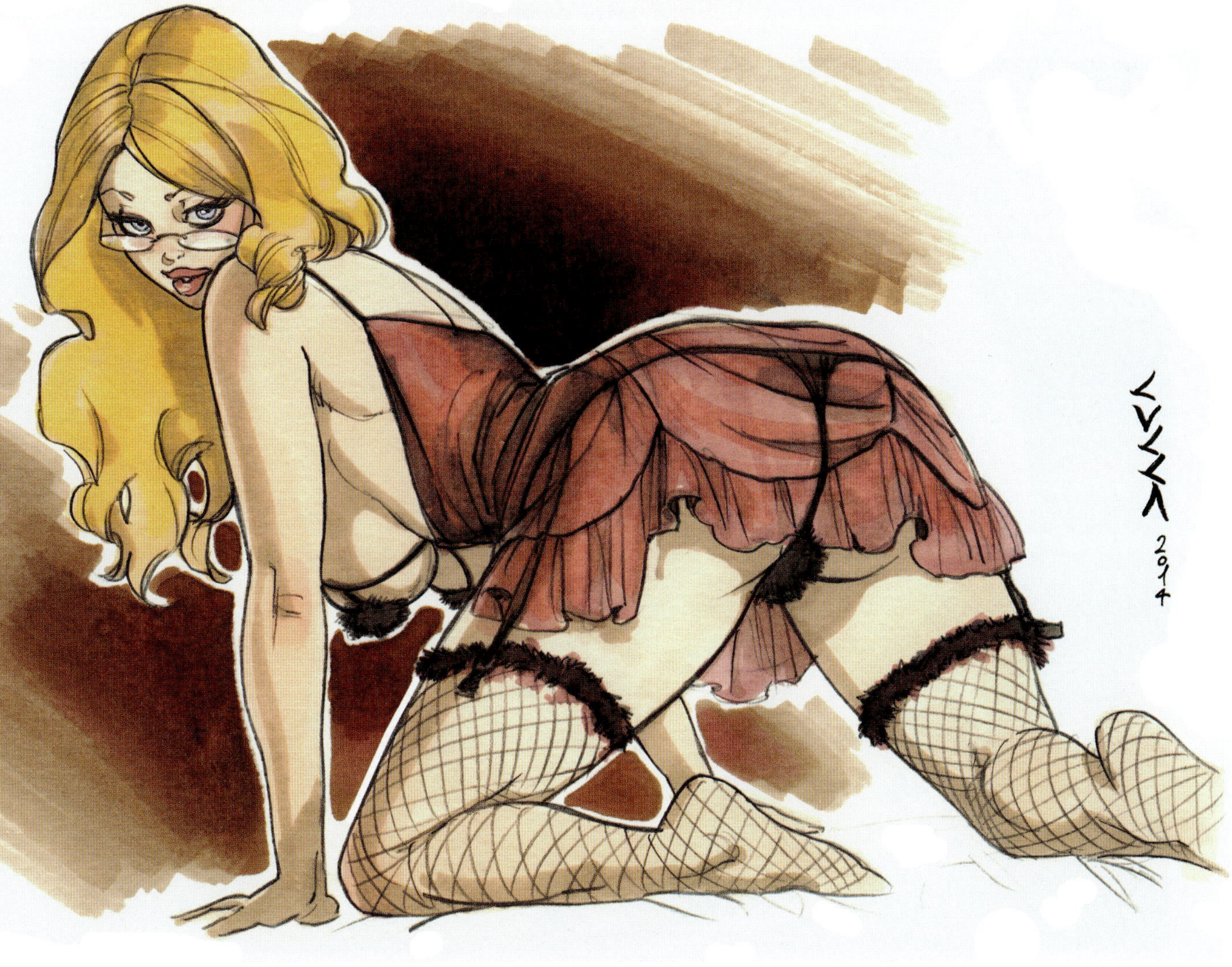

What Are You Waiting For?

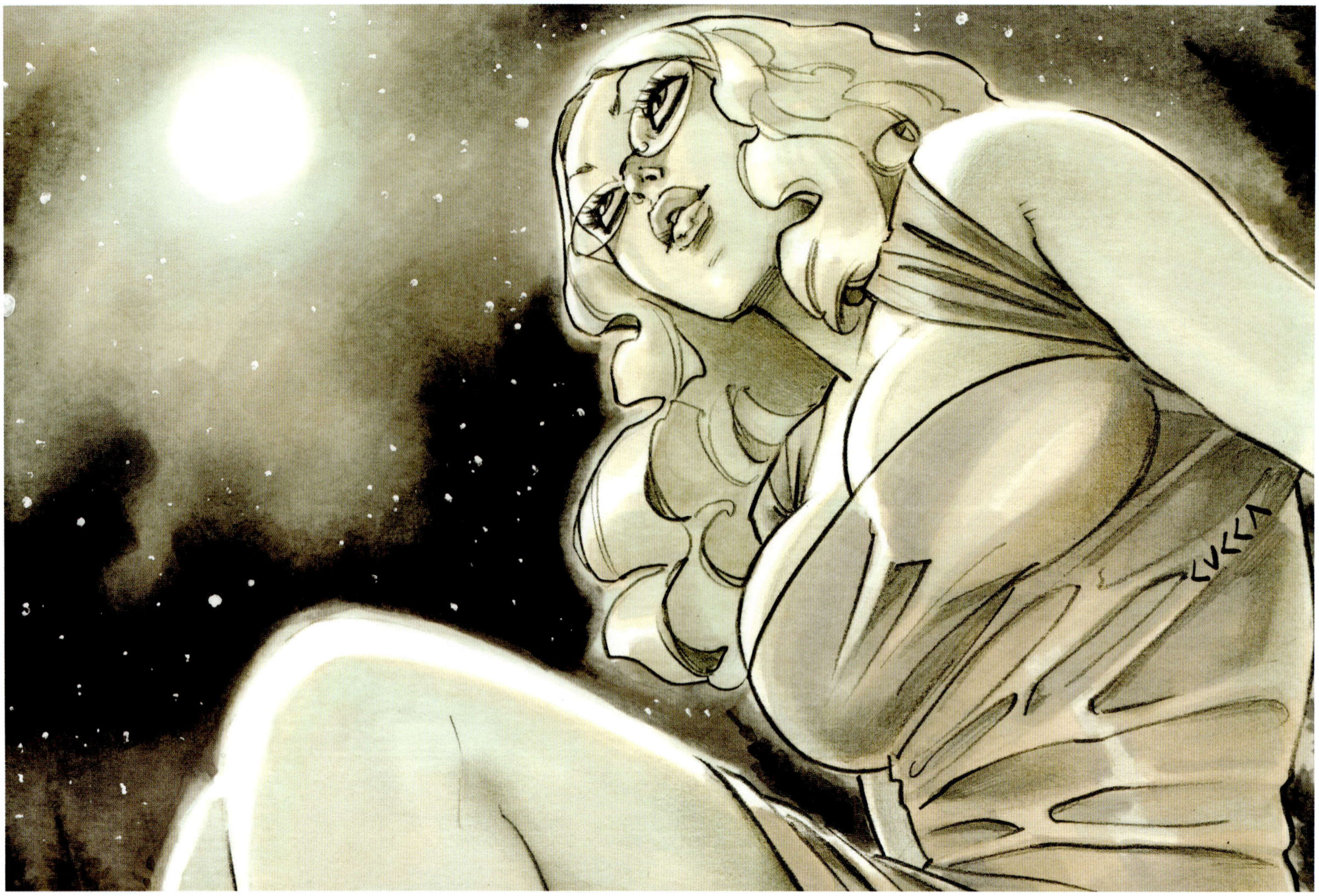

Charlotte By Night

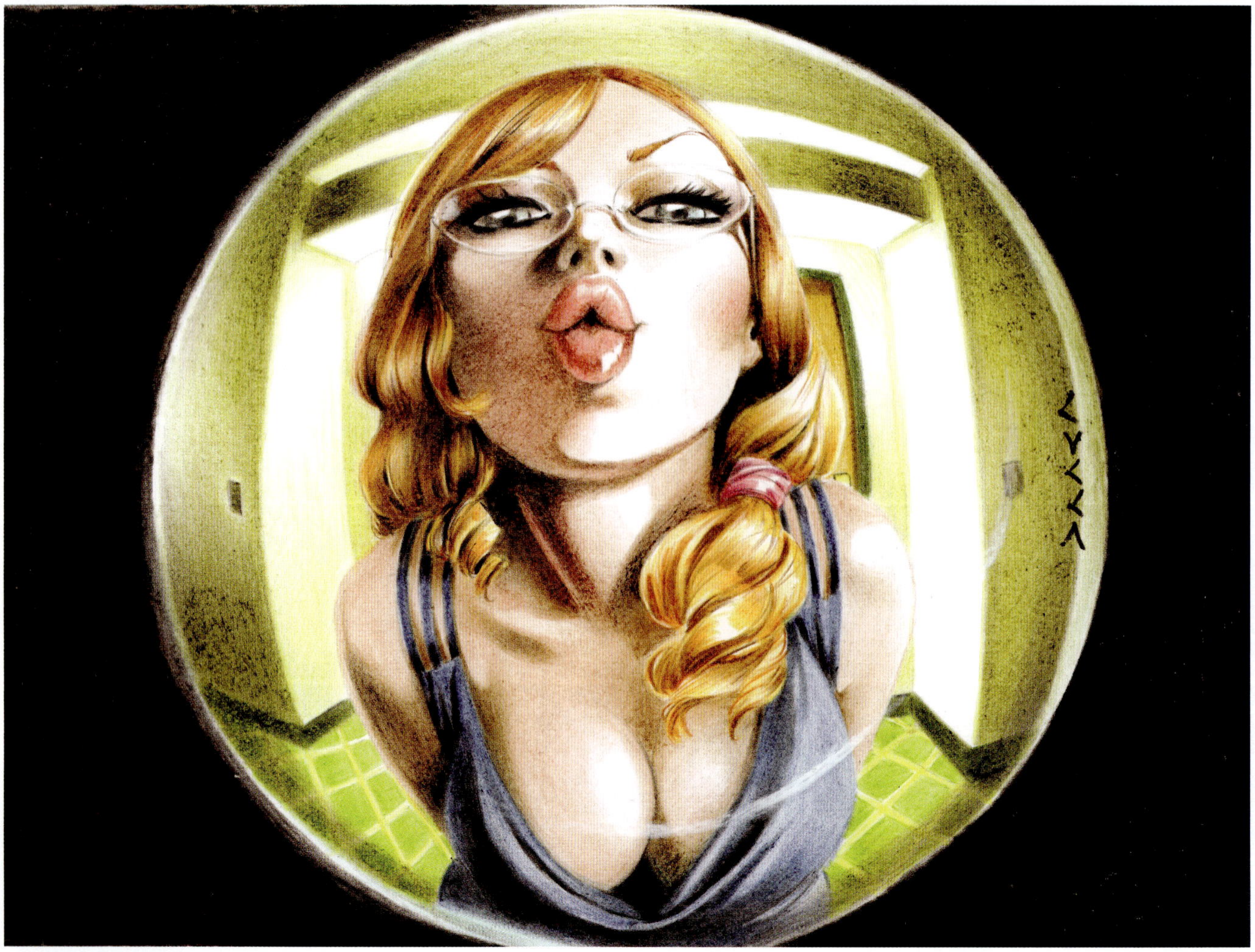

Best Reason To Open The Door

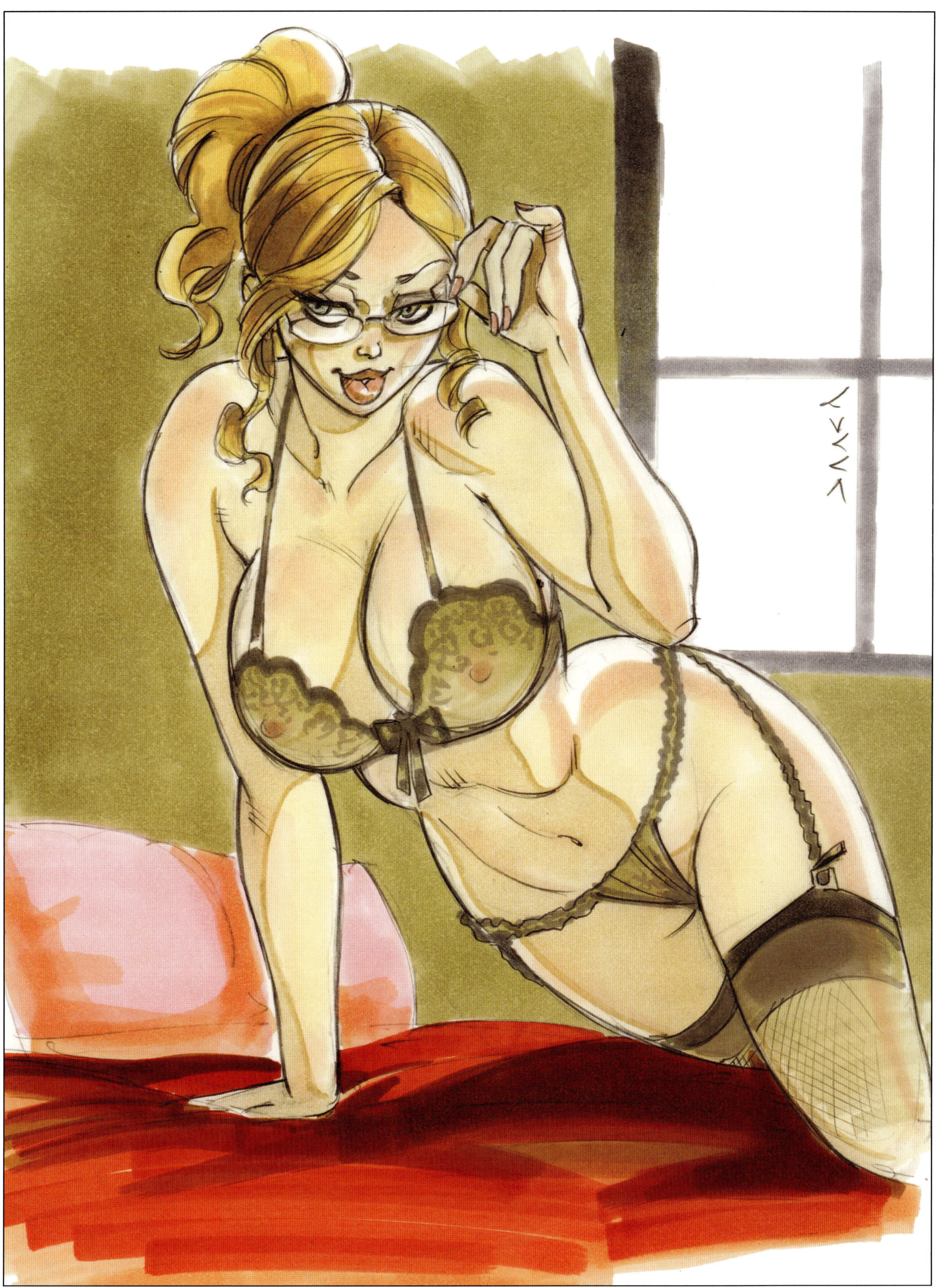

In The Mood

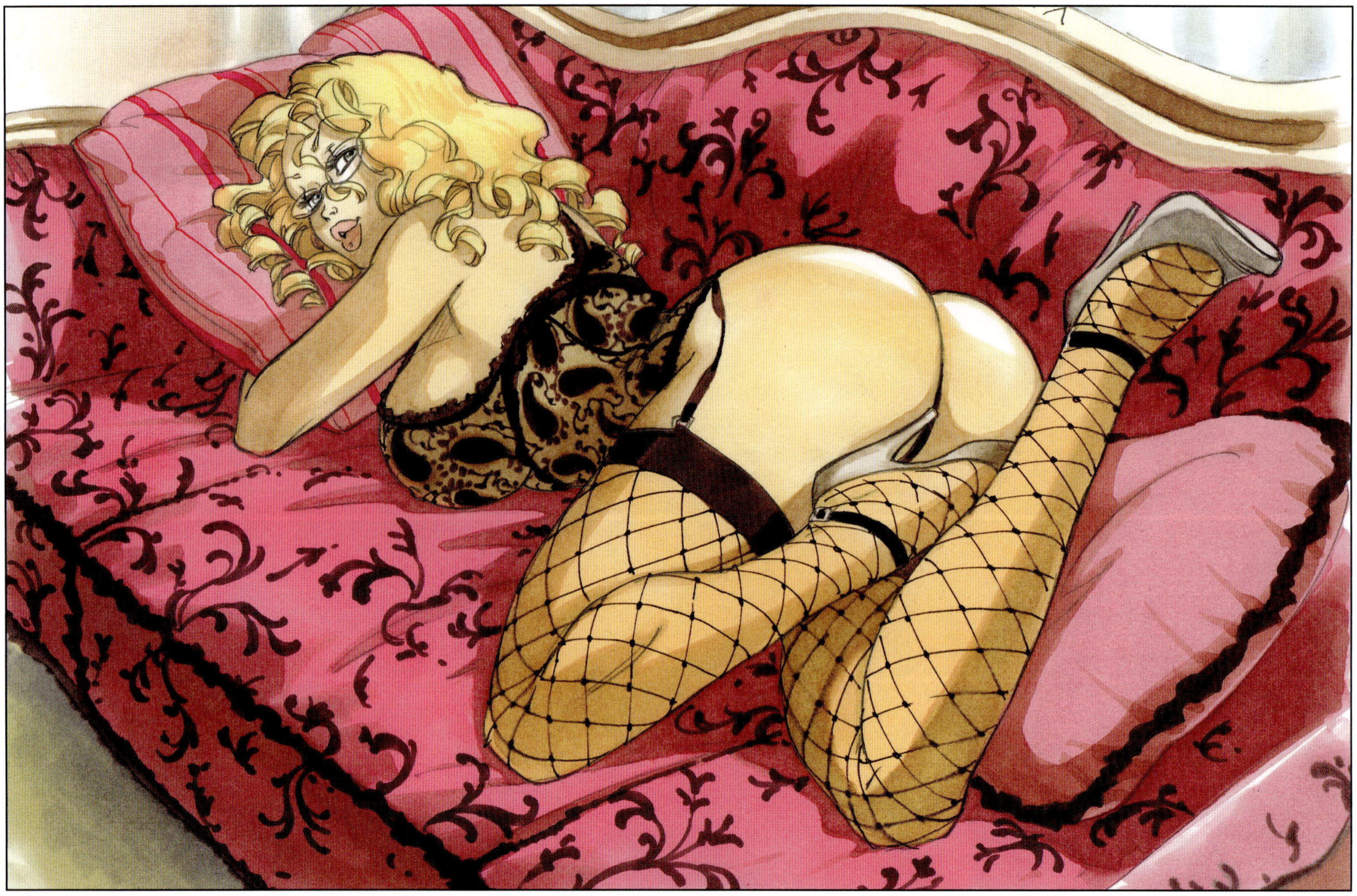

Caught Me Napping

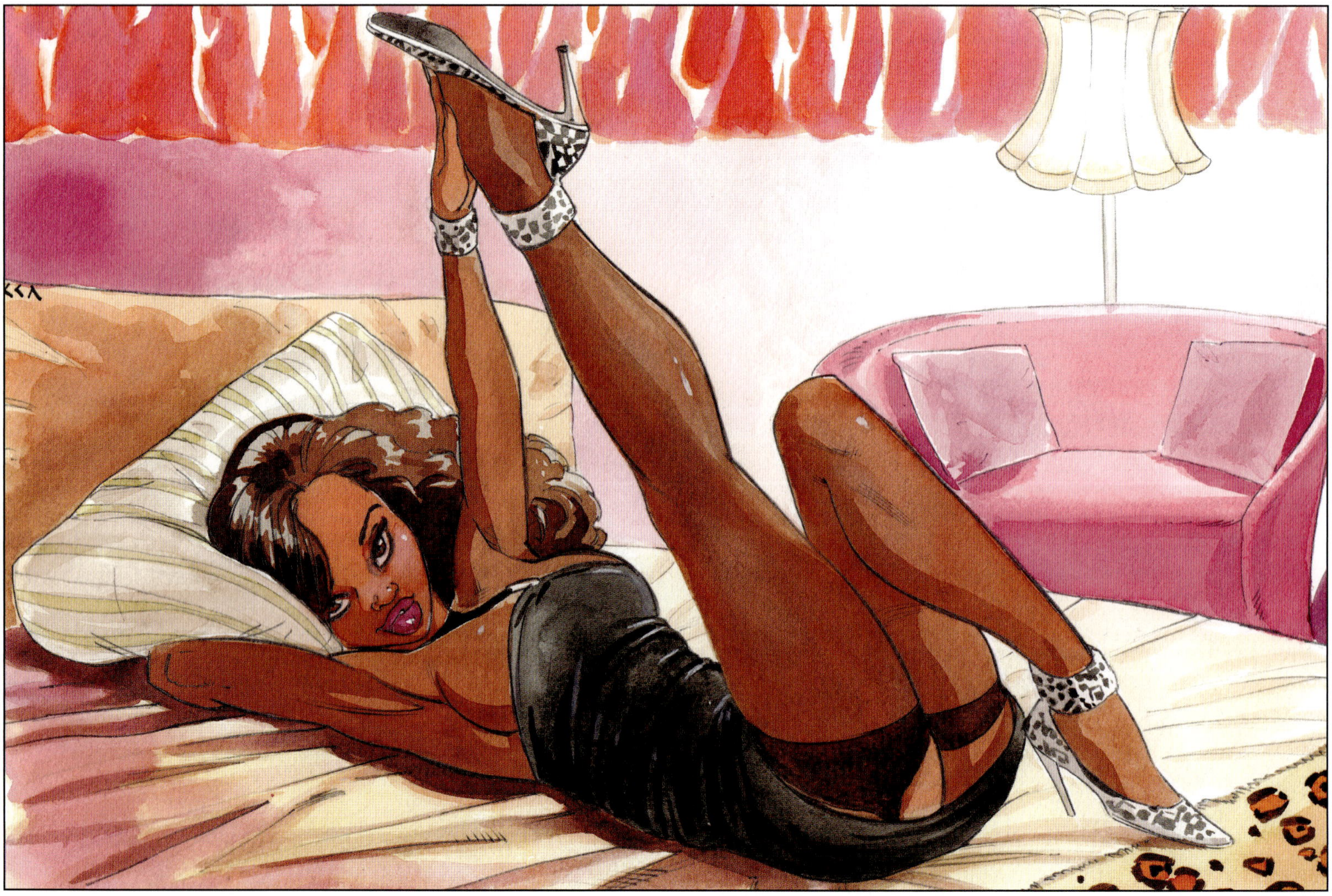

You Like The New Shoes?

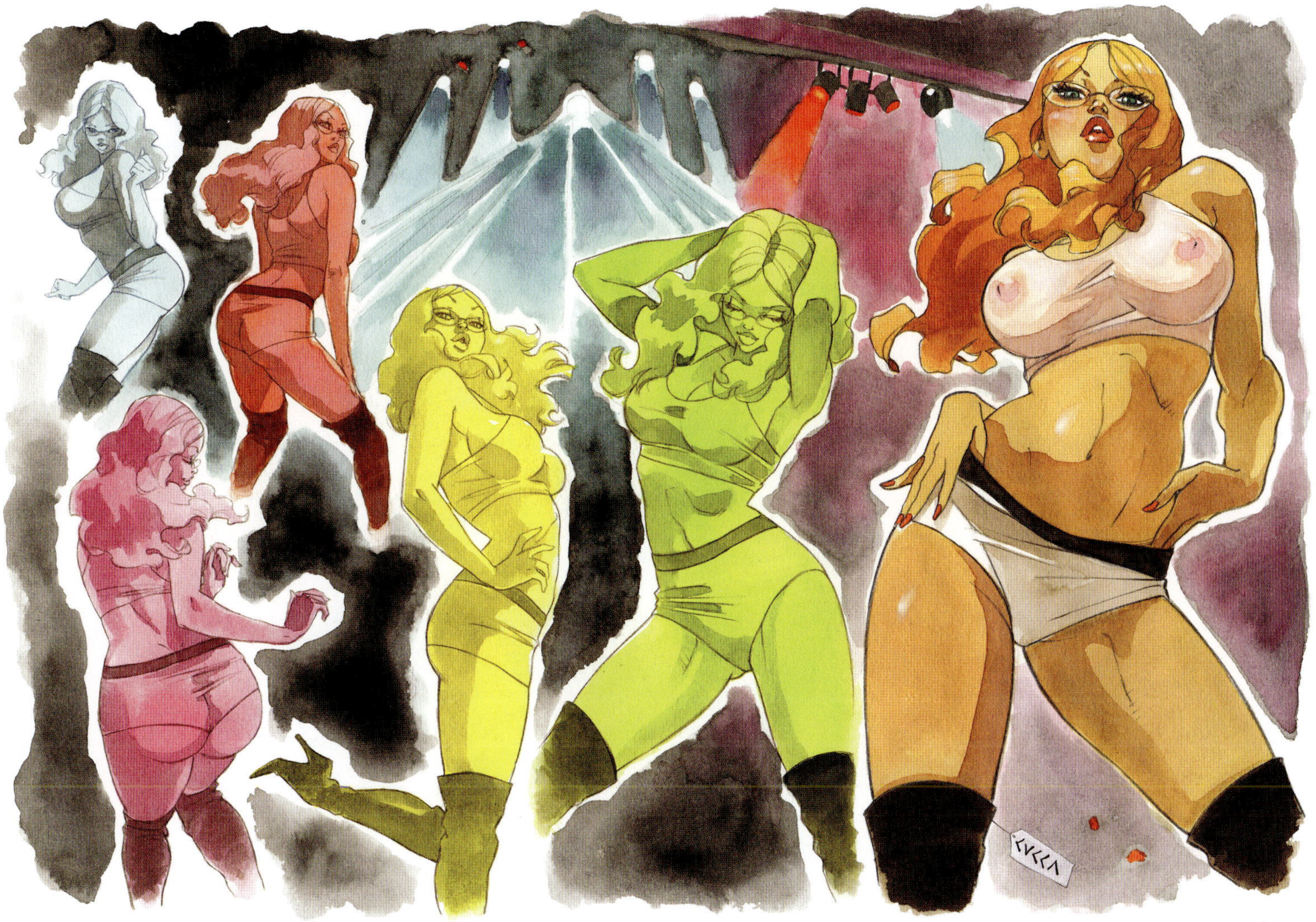

Pump Up The Jam

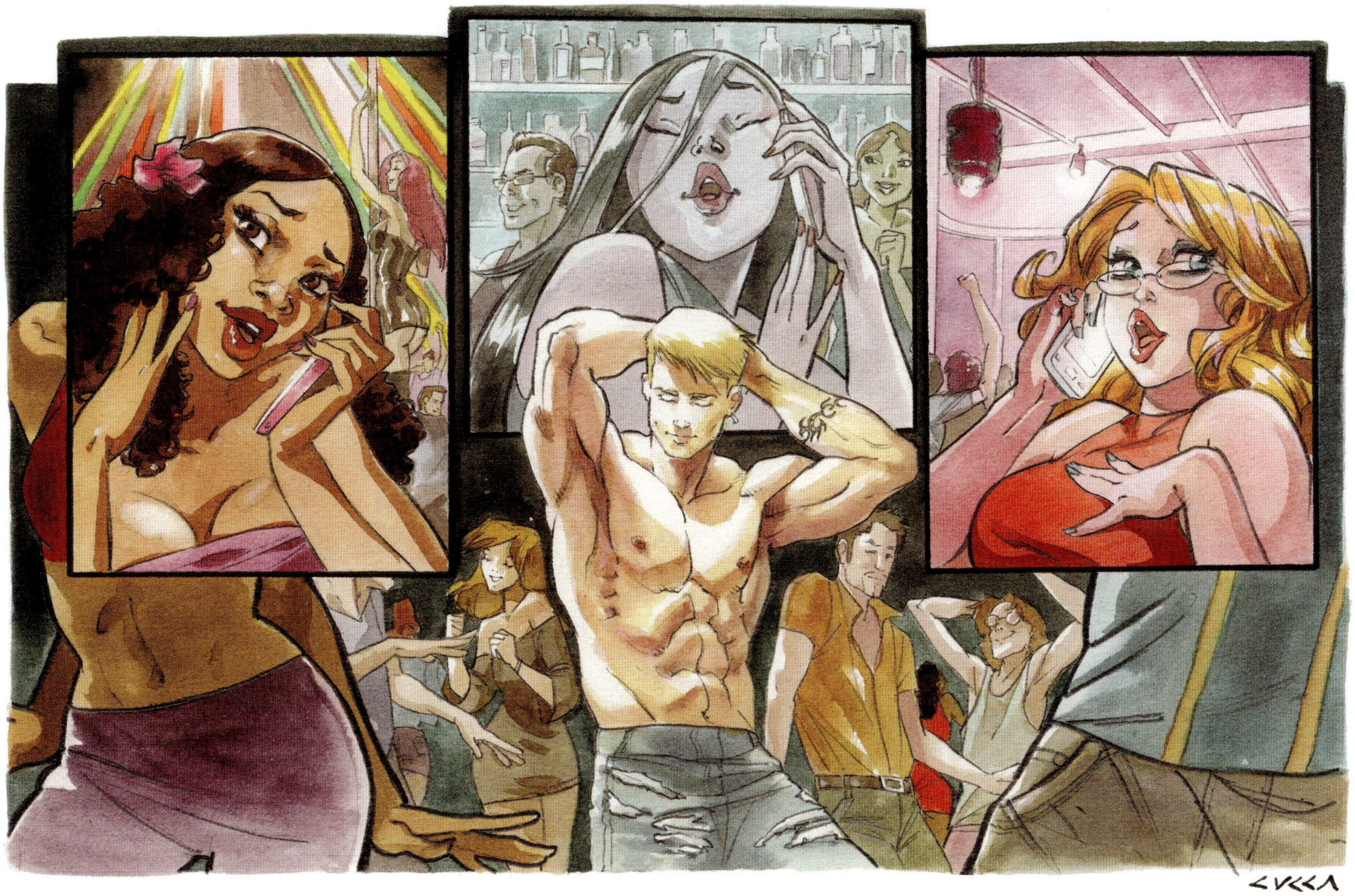

Object of Affections

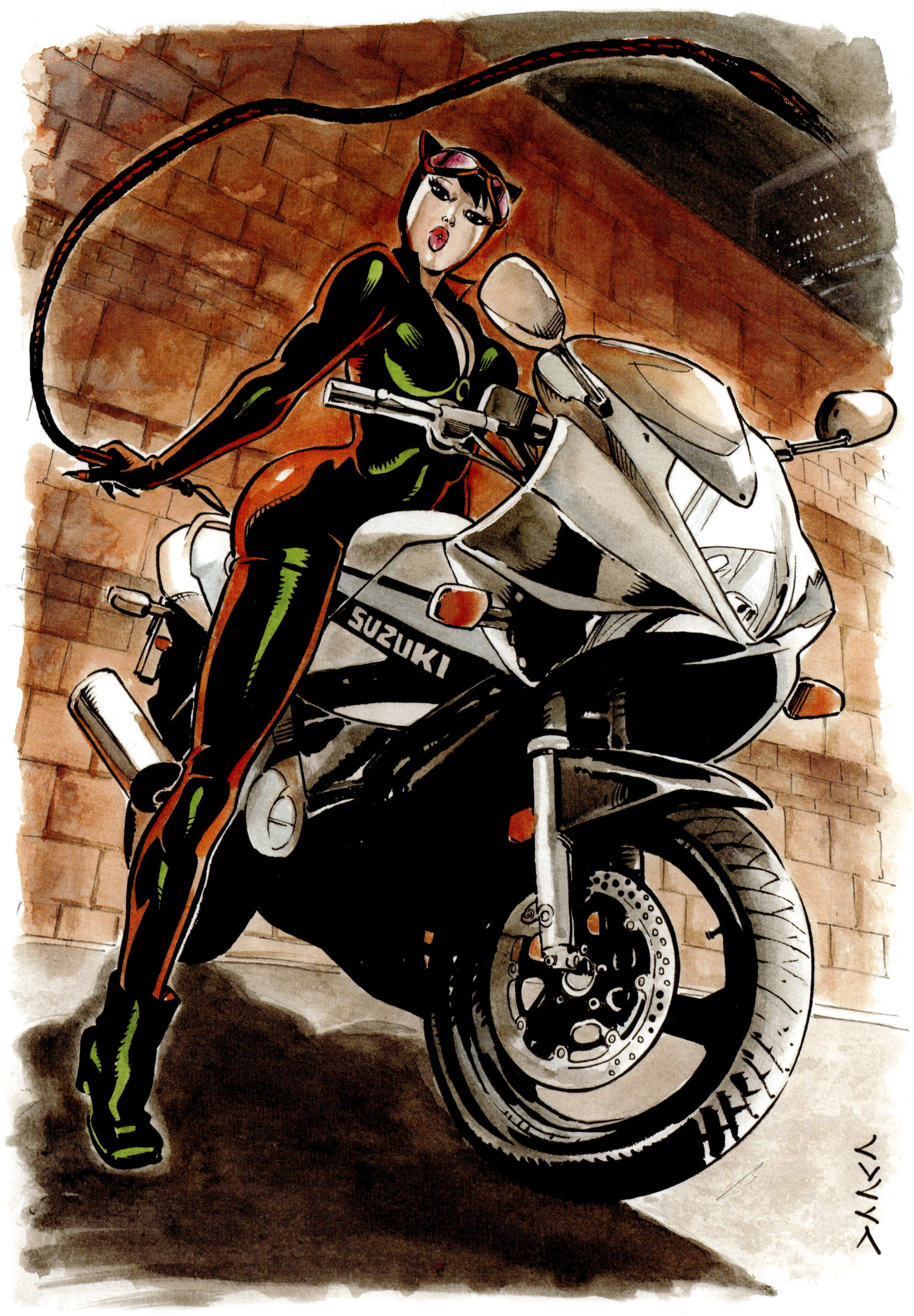

Yes, I Stole This Ride

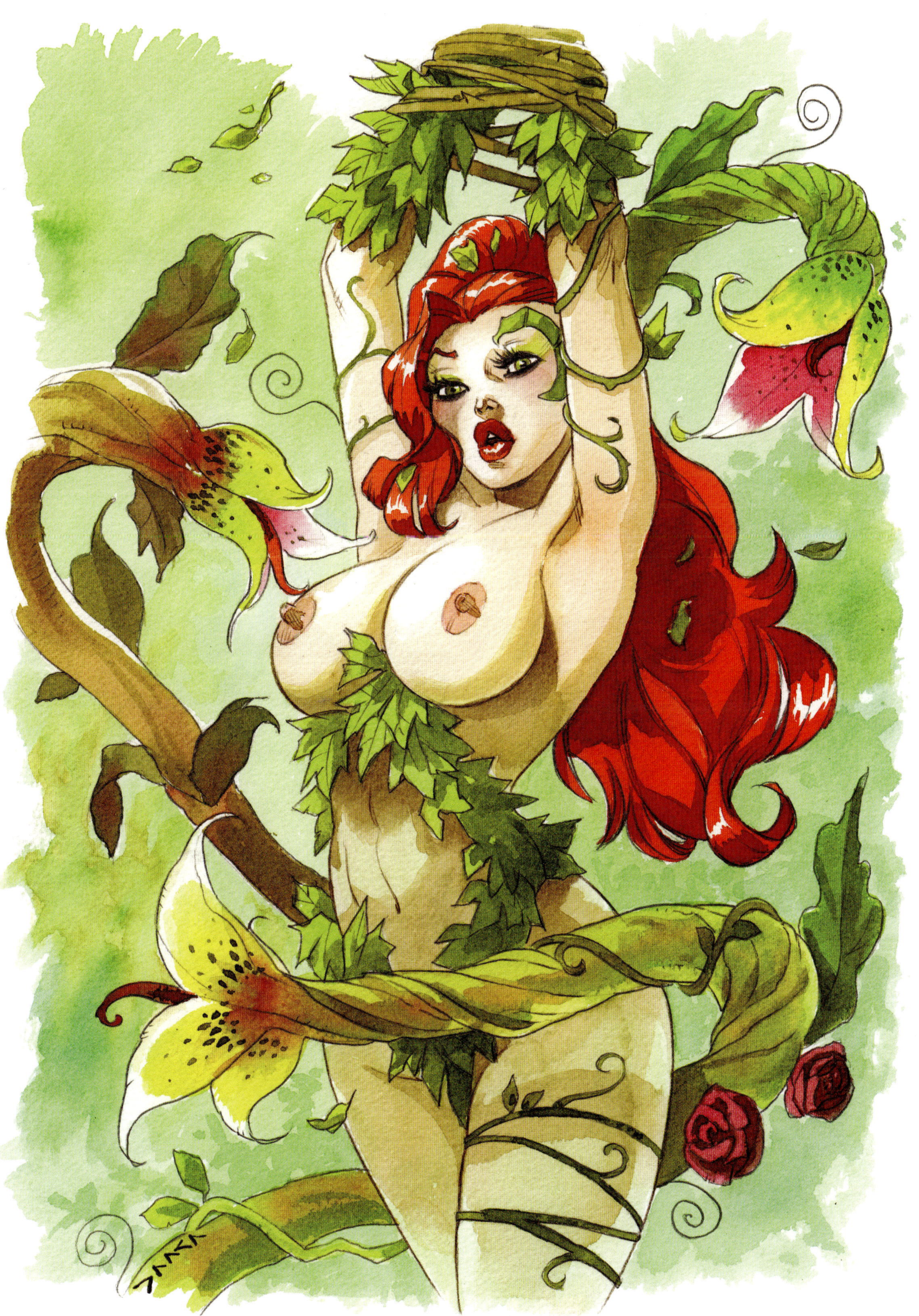

Nature's Plaything

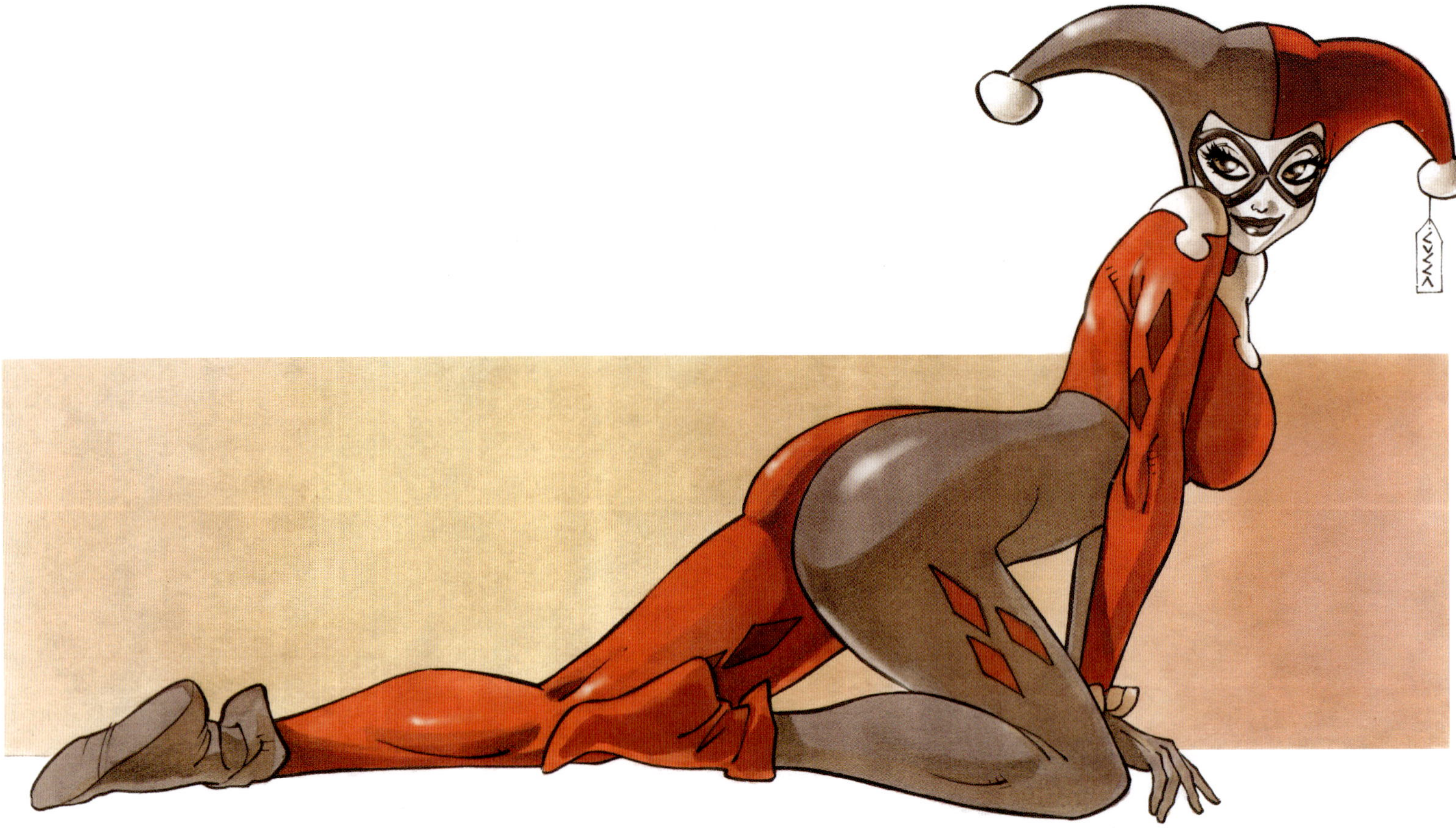

Mistah J's Squeeze

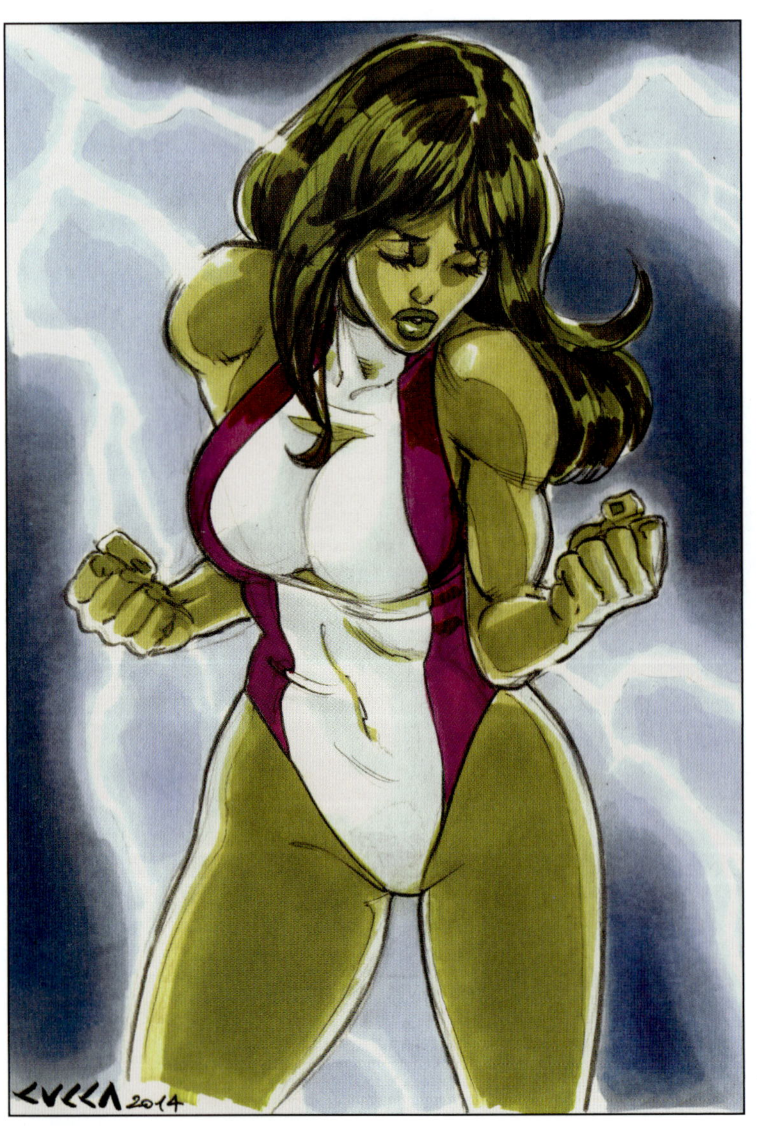

Gamma Glamour

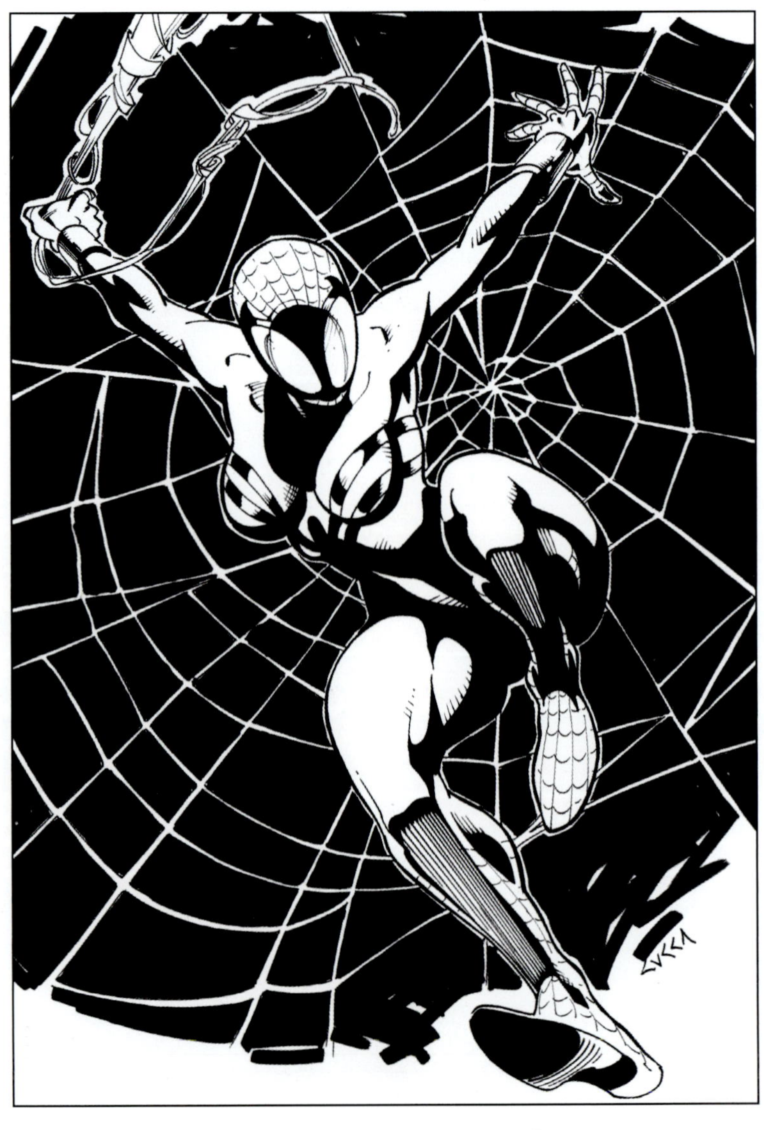

"With Great Curves..."

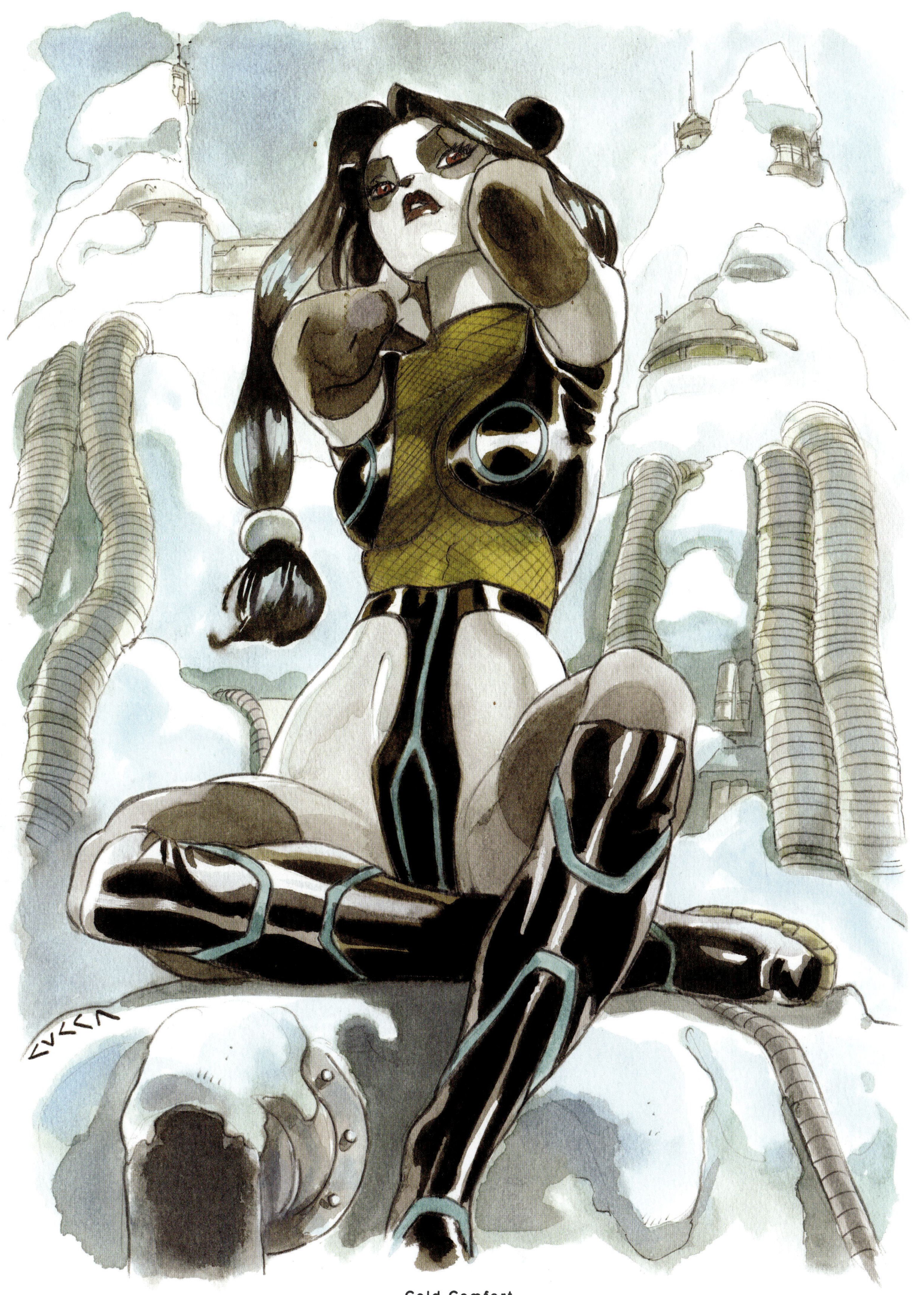

Cold Comfort

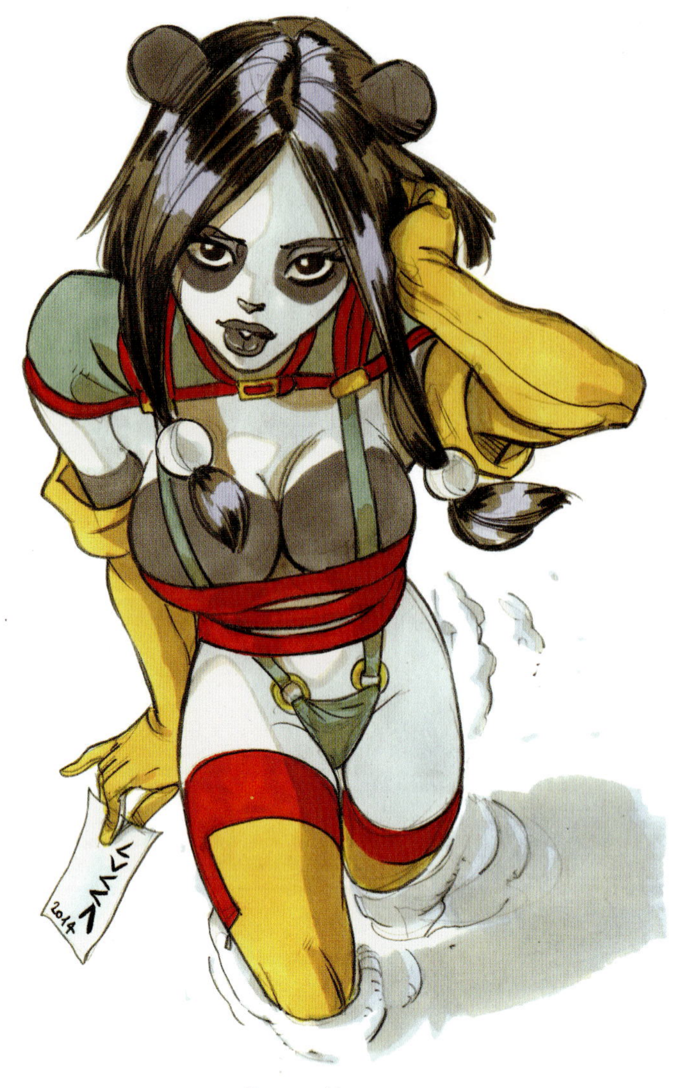

Snow Honey

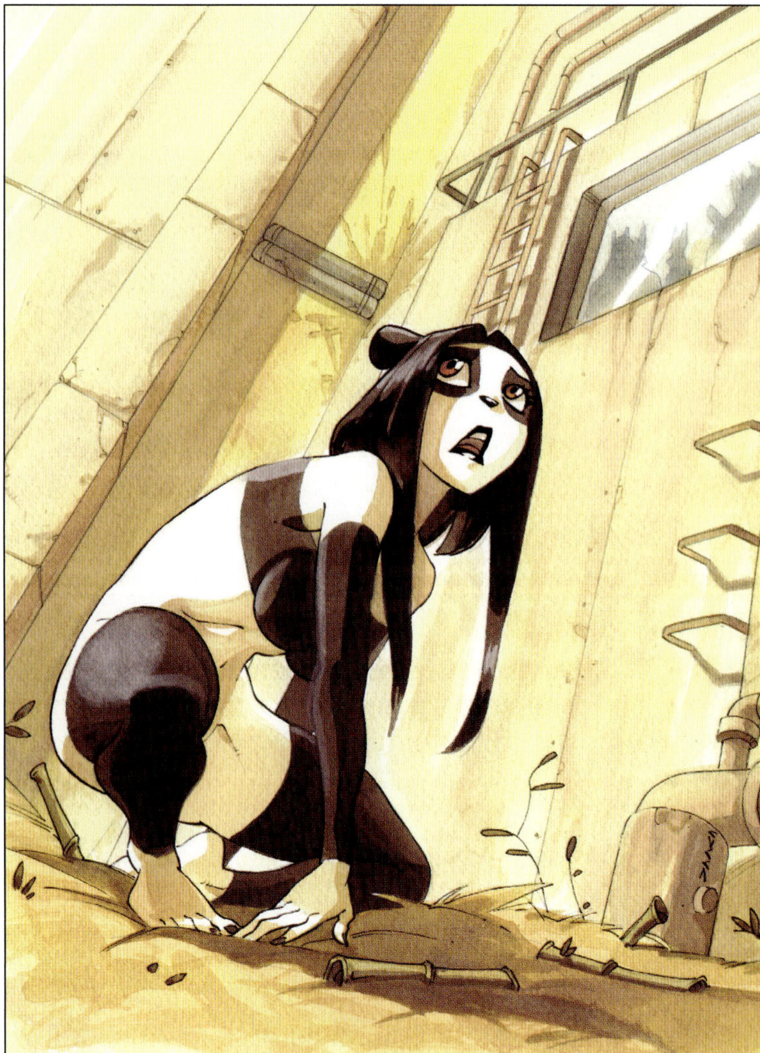

Trapped

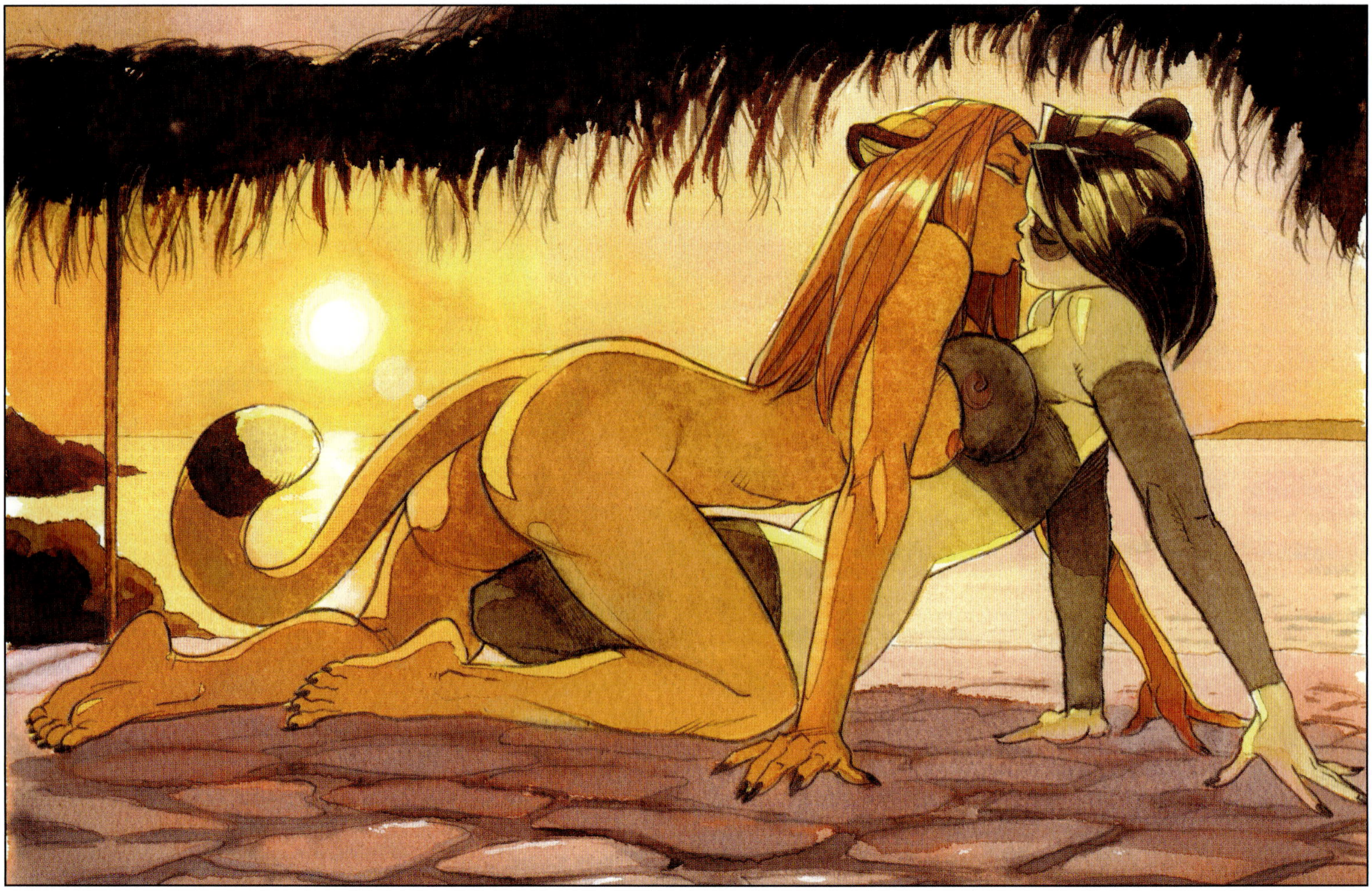

Sunset Kiss

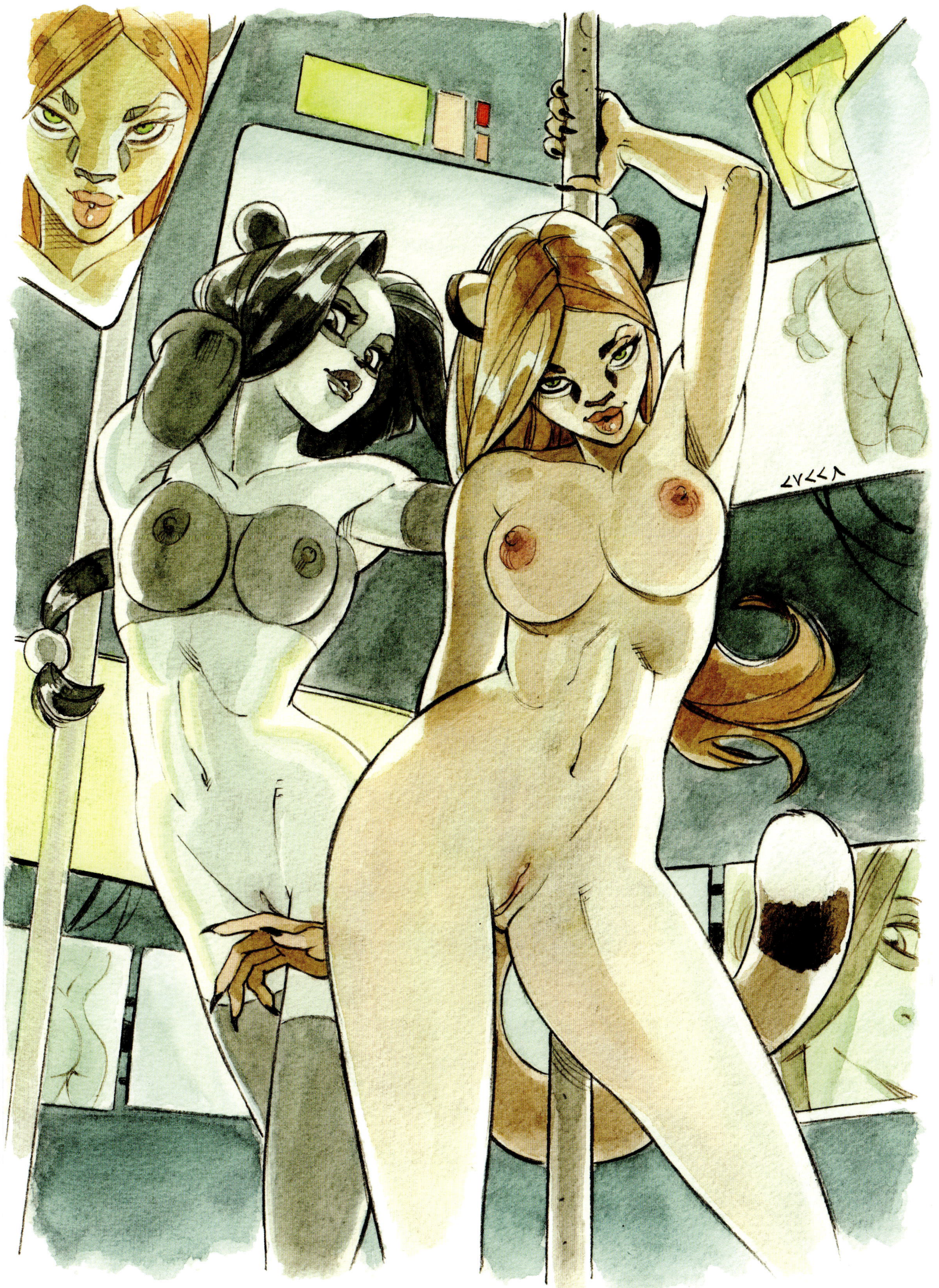

Erotic Exotic Dancers

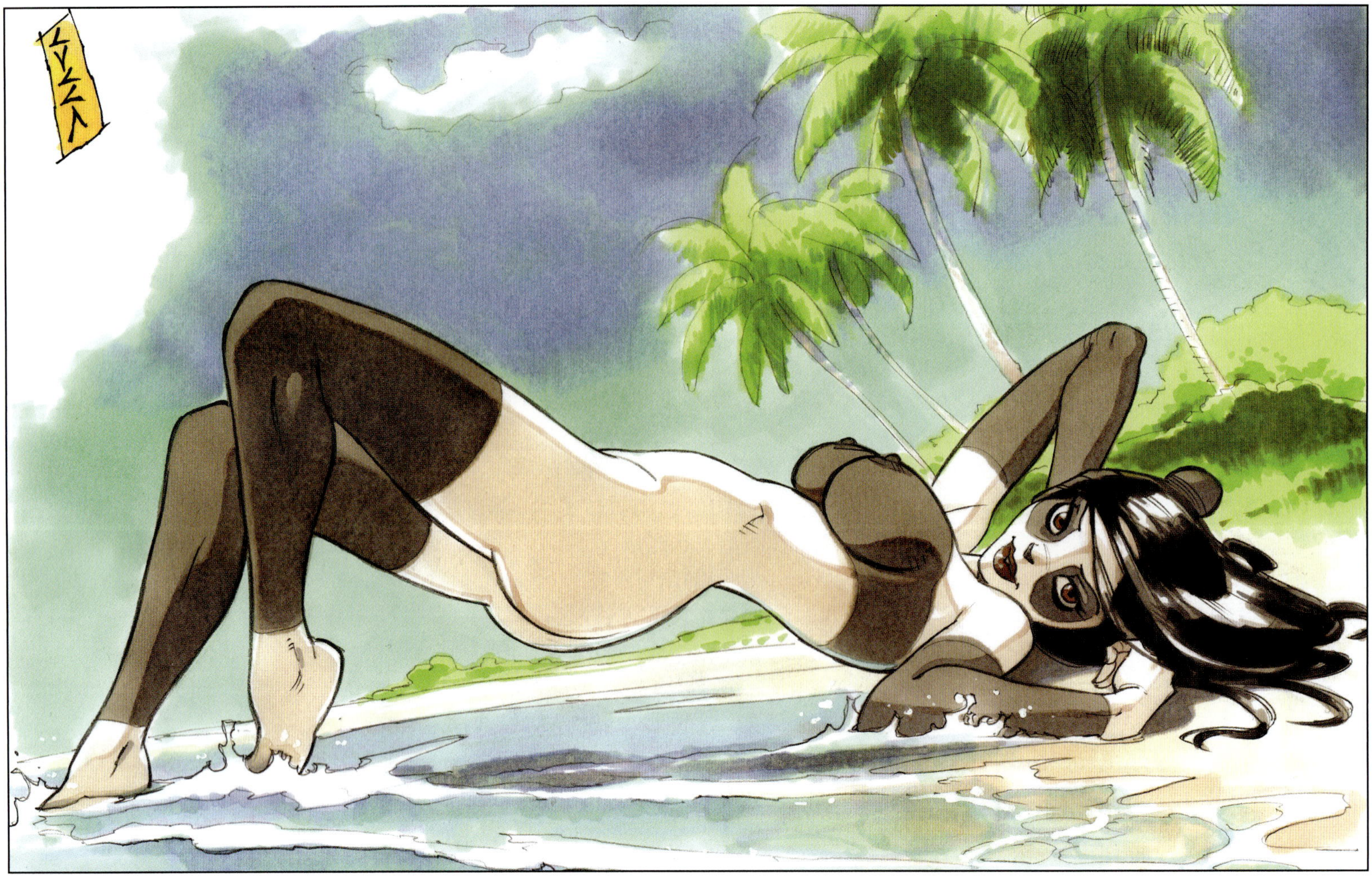

Vanessa's Summer

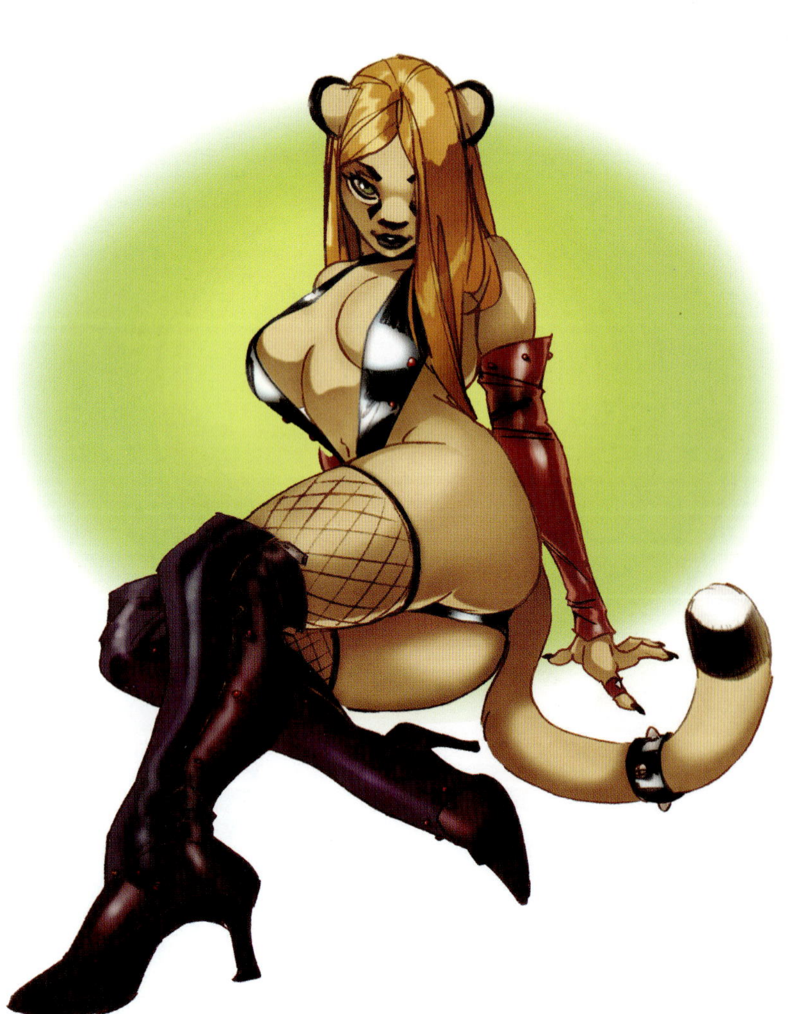

Susanna

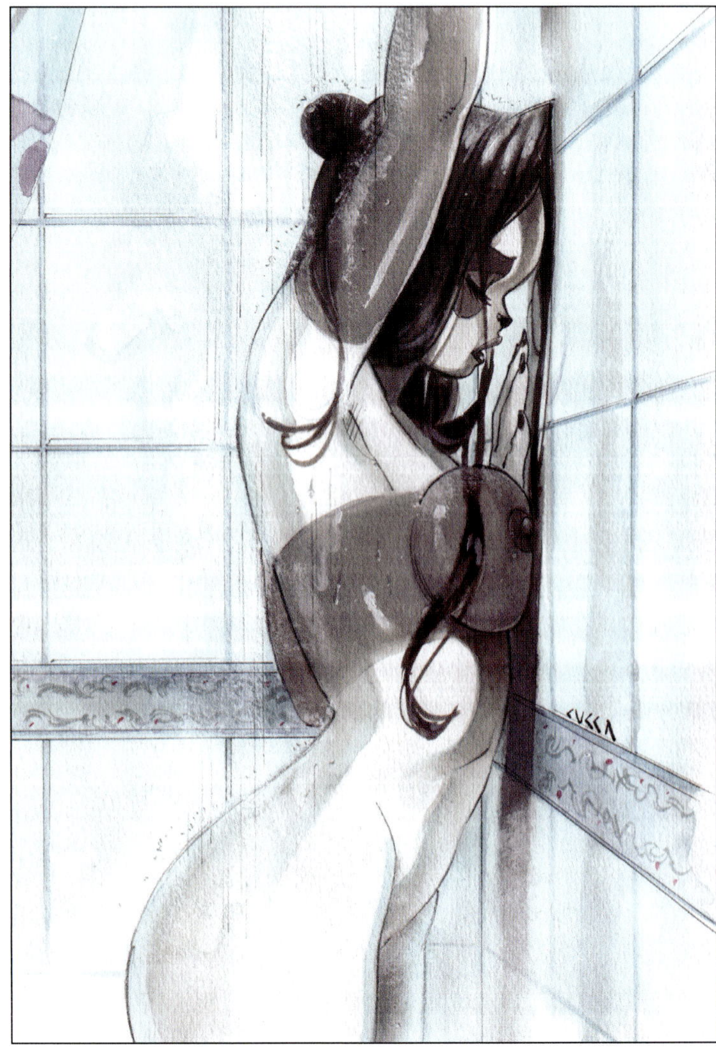

Wash It All Away

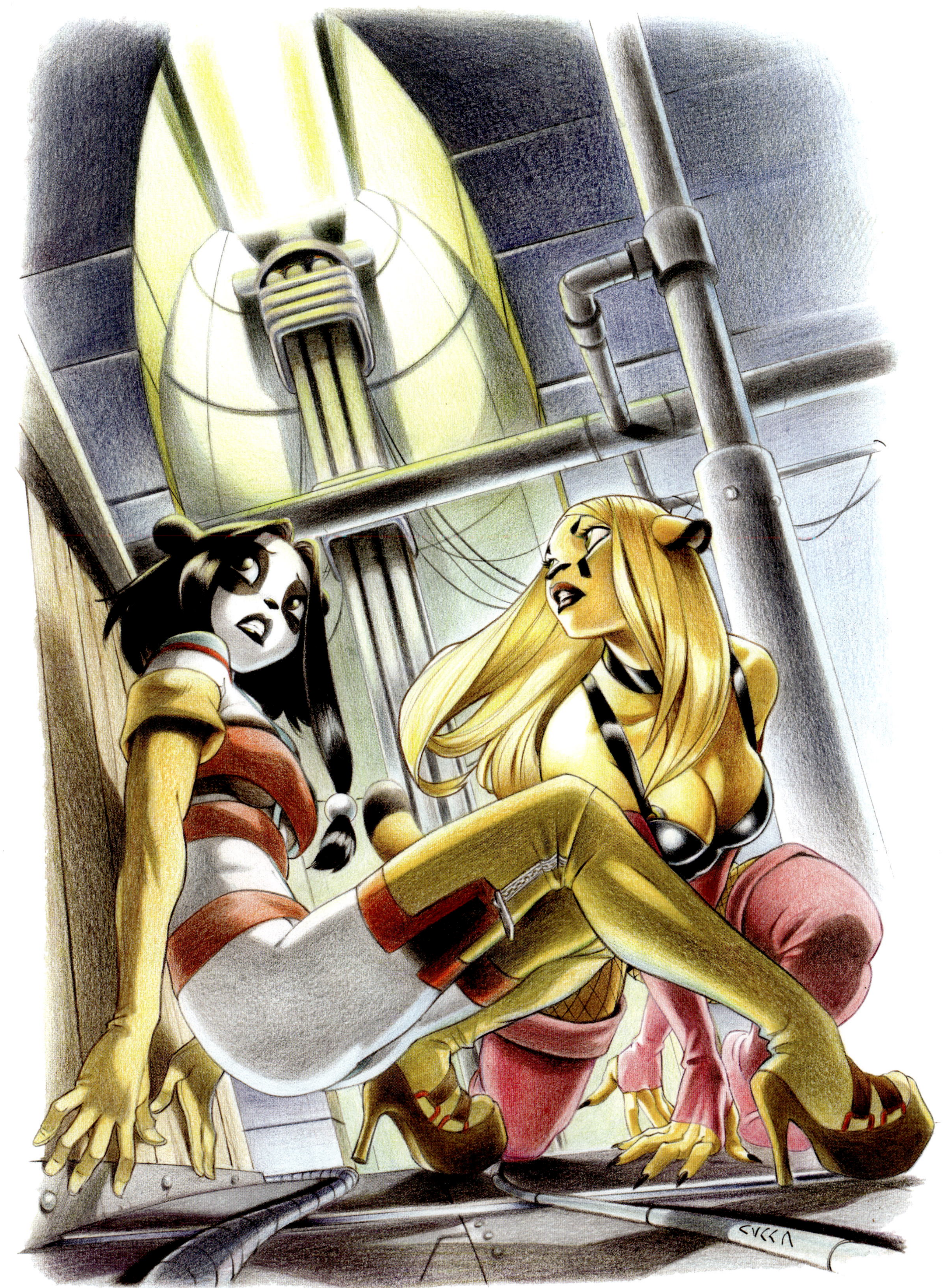

On The Run

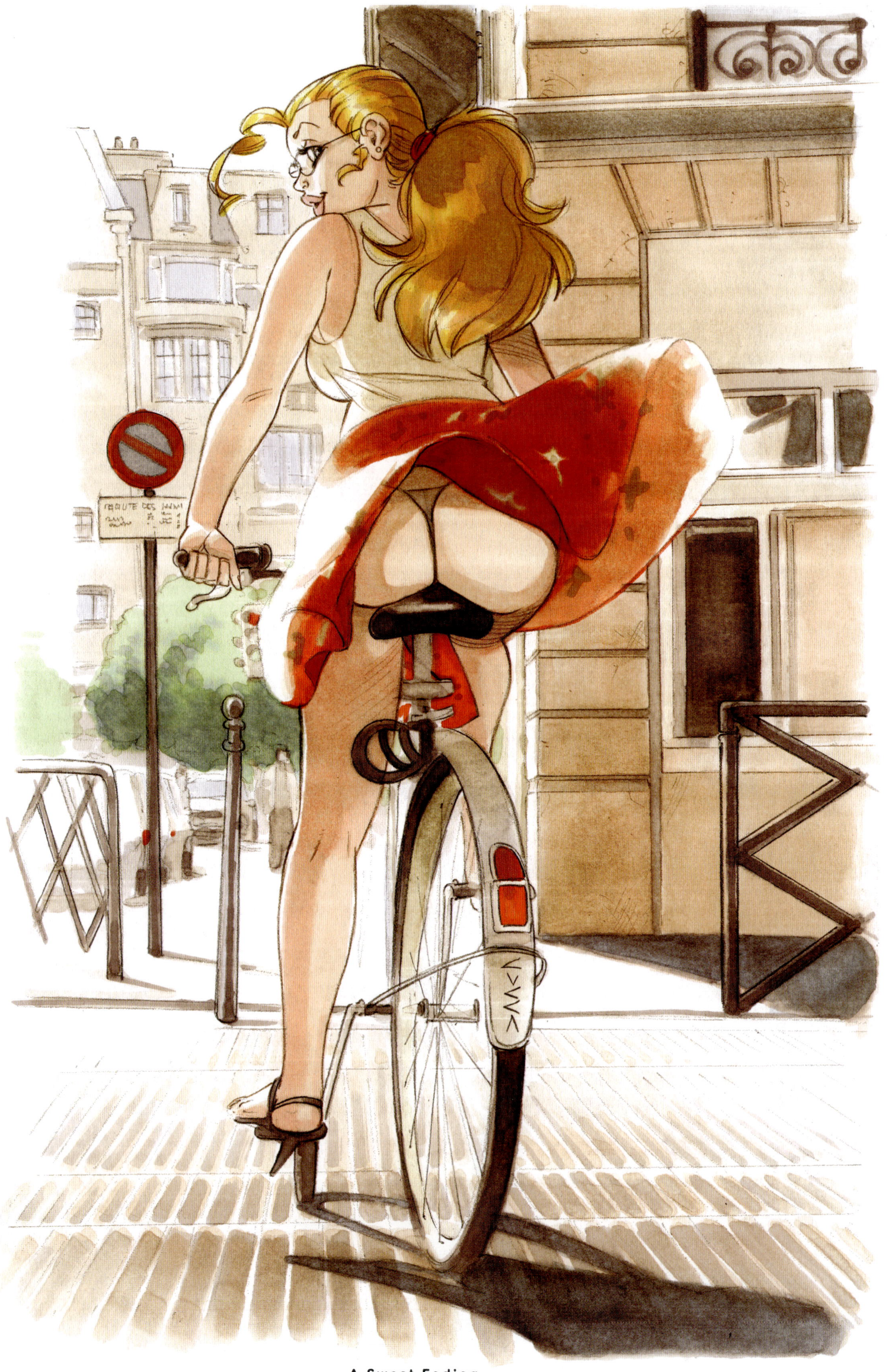

A Sweet Ending